STOP
CHASING
HAPPINESS

Frank Martela, PhD, is a philosopher, assistant professor and researcher of psychology at Aalto University in Finland, specializing in happiness, meaningfulness, human motivation, and how organizations and institutions can unleash human potential. He has lectured at universities around the world, and his last book *A Wonderful Life – Insights on Finding a Meaningful Experience* (HarperCollins, 2020) was translated into twenty-nine languages. Frank is a key authority on why Finland is so happy, having written extensively on Nordic well-being, alongside being the Principal Investigator for a research team developing a well-being module for European Social Survey 2025.

FRANK MARTELA

STOP CHASING HAPPINESS

A pessimist's guide to a good life

ALLEN&UNWIN

Published in hardback in Great Britain in 2025 by Allen & Unwin,
an imprint of Atlantic Books Ltd.

10 9 8 7 6 5 4 3 2

A CIP catalogue record for this book is available from the British Library.

Hardback ISBN: 978 1 80546 373 3
E-book ISBN: 978 1 80546 374 0

Printed in India by Replika Press Pvt. Ltd.

Atlantic Books
An imprint of Atlantic Books Ltd
Ormond House
26–27 Boswell Street
London
WCIN 3JZ

www.atlantic-books.co.uk

Product safety EU representative: Authorised Rep Compliance Ltd., Ground Floor,
71 Lower Baggot Street, Dublin, D02 P593, Ireland. www.arccompliance.com

CONTENTS

Introduction: Are You Ready to Be Born for the Third Time?   1

PART I: Kill the Ego

Chapter 1: Stop Caring About Your Own Happiness   17

Chapter 2: Stop Caring About What Others Think   29

Chapter 3: Stop Caring About How You Feel   49

PART II: Kill the Expectations

Chapter 4: Stop Caring About Your Past   73

Chapter 5: Stop Caring About What Happens in the World   85

Chapter 6: Stop Caring About Your Future Success   99

INTERMISSION

Chapter 7: The Centre of Indifference   121

PART III: Start Living Your Own Life

Chapter 8: Start Caring About Yourself   133

Chapter 9: Start Caring About Others   157

Chapter 10: Start Caring About Building a Better World   169

Conclusion: The Delicate Art of Not Caring, While Caring Deeply   181

Acknowledgements   195

Notes   199

———

ARE YOU READY TO BE BORN FOR THE THIRD TIME?

I was twenty-four and living the dream as an exchange student in Thailand. Together with my classmates, I spent the weekends (which lasted four days as we didn't have lectures on Fridays or Mondays) at beach resorts, sleeping in cheap bungalows, drinking buckets of vodka mixed with energy drinks and dancing on the beach until sunrise. Other nights were spent in the most luxurious nightclubs of Bangkok, where the buying power of Western salaries meant that it really felt like the world was our oyster. The bars were our temples, and we felt like gods, living the kind of dream life that we thought only existed in music videos.

I was young and it was, of course, a hell of a lot of fun. But as one weekend of shenanigans followed another, a nagging feeling began to grow. I started to realize I was living in someone else's dream. This was the lifestyle that advertisements, music videos and movies had programmed us to enjoy. *This was supposed to be the dream life.* But while it was fun, I felt that I was missing out on something. A sense of emptiness started to trouble me. Eventually, I realized that I was missing the 'boring' parts of life, like reading and writing. It dawned on me that the way of living best suited for who I truly was involved more books, not more beach parties.

So I went to the university library. I read philosophical classics like Friedrich Nietzsche and William James. At some hippie bookshop on a beach in Koh Pha-ngan, I found a worn copy of Viktor Frankl's *Man's Search for Meaning*. Then and there, during the most hedonic period of my youth, I decided that what I wanted to do in life was to solve the riddle of human happiness. What makes our lives happy, fulfilling and meaningful? And, ultimately, what should we strive for in life?

In the decade that followed, I graduated, started and completed my PhD, found a person to love in sickness and in health, had three lovely children with her and found my calling in research, publishing both psychological and philosophical works on the grand questions of life. Beyond this, I travelled to six continents, interviewing and having a few beers with people from all walks of life and gaining experiences – all in the service of acquiring a deeper understanding of what living a good life entails for us humans.

When Finland was crowned the happiest nation on earth for the first time in 2018, I realized that what I had been looking for had been hiding in plain sight. Perhaps the secret to good living was not to be found on the beaches of Belize, in the bungee jumping in New Zealand, in Singapore, Silicon Valley, Winchester, or even in the psychology department of the University of Rochester in upstate New

York, where I spent a year and a half as a visiting researcher. The secret was waiting for me where I had started: at home. At the time of writing, Finland has topped the rankings of the World Happiness Report for seven years in a row, leading to journalists from all over the world trying to figure out how this tiny Nordic country with long and cold winters can have such happy citizens. Consequently, as a Finnish wellbeing researcher, I've been sharing my take on Finnish happiness with media from all over the world, including the *New York Times*, BBC, CNN, and even Fox News.

Our secret? Finns don't care too much about happiness. When the country was first nominated the happiest nation, the overall reaction in Finland was one of disbelief and scepticism. The people of the land of darkness, heavy metal and valorized melancholy, where winter is always coming, were not ready to believe it to be true. But it is – I've researched the topic for over a decade and have been able to convince many Finns that they, indeed, are happy. I see Finland as the *land of quiet satisfaction* – people accept life as it is, not making a fuss about what is bad or good in their life. But at the end of the day, when pushed to answer, they admit that they are actually quite satisfied with their lives. The art of accepting life as it is is something wisdom traditions all over the world – from Stoicism and Taoism to Buddhism – have taught us. And, in Finland, people have taken this message to heart.

However, contentment in the present is just half the story. You also need excitement for the future. A healthy human life is not one of passive satisfaction, but of active engagement – you need goals and values, the pursuit of which energizes your present. Being *content* with what you have should not lead you to *settle* with what you have – that is a recipe for boredom. We need challenges and goals to stretch ourselves; we need something to look forward to. The trick to good living is the ability to hold these two seemingly contradictory attitudes simultaneously: accepting the present unconditionally, while pursuing goals and projects you find valuable. This is the attitude of *energized contentment* that I will be offering to you in this book.

At the end of the day, happiness is not about some grand mind tricks or external signs of success. It is about an attitude towards life. Learning to approach life with energized contentment is mostly about unlearning harmful attitudes and unhealthy cultural norms that stand in the way of your happiness. As Brené Brown puts it, we can talk about the good things in life 'until we sound like a greeting card store', but such well-meaning 'how-to' advice does not help, because 'I've never seen any evidence of "how-to" working without talking about the things that get in the way.'[1] On our way to unconditionally accepting life as it is, we have to deal with how we approach our past, how we approach our future, how we deal with our emotions and setbacks, and what others think of us. In the end, we also have to deal with how we approach happiness itself and what our attitude towards our own happiness is. All of this is necessary groundwork for clearing the way for being able to combine acceptance *and* excitement towards life.

So, if unconditional acceptance of the present combined with excitedly pursuing whatever project you have chosen for yourself sounds like something you would like to master in your own life, let's go on a journey together!

Do You Dare to Liberate Yourself?

What if I offered you a life that is not about jumping through hoops in the pursuit of a carrot you did not choose?

This is a book about liberation – about letting go of the false attachments that keep us anchored in life courses and choices that are harmful to us. We are entangled in a web of expectations, prejudices and fears that keep us trapped in a narrow path. In the worst-case scenario, you are stuck doing work that you don't like, to get money to buy stuff you don't need, to impress people you don't care about. This book aims to set you free.

I will not promise you success. I will not promise you riches. I will not promise that your problems will go away. Putting into practice the insights in the following pages will make these outcomes more likely – so, this book is not *against* success – but this is a book that aims to change your perspective so that success becomes a nice potential side effect, not the end goal of life.

What I promise you is perspective. The ability to deal better with whatever you are dealing with. The capacity to more energetically pursue whatever it is you want to pursue. And, most of all, I promise you self-awareness – the wisdom to know what is worth pursuing in life (and, just as importantly, what is not). The goal is to make you love your life as it is, while being excited to pursue what you value.

The aim is to stop living a life where you are just a commodity, just an instrument for something else, such as success, fame, a productive career or being accepted by others. Whatever you come to pursue in life through reading this book, I want it to be something you chose yourself and something that you personally value.

I want to make you live more alertly, more reflectively, more freely and, ultimately, more fully.

Existentialism for People with Baggage

In being a book about liberation, there is a strong strain of existentialism running through these pages. Existentialism was a movement of philosophers and artists that aimed to awaken people to the notion that they are free and should thus start living more authentically.[2] The German Friedrich Nietzsche, Russian Fyodor Dostoevsky and Danish Søren Kierkegaard are often quoted as the nineteenth-century predecessors of existentialism, while post-World War II France was the epicentre of the movement, with Jean-Paul Sartre, Simone de Beauvoir and Albert Camus leading the charge. In Finland, philosopher Esa Saarinen has been at the forefront of nudging people to start steering their own lives. From a young 'punk doctor' in leather trousers in the 1980s to a professor of life philosophy in leopard-patterned suits in the 2000s, he still draws full lecture halls and his videos gather hundreds of thousands of views on YouTube – not bad for two-hour-long university lectures. As Esa's former PhD student and mentee, it is my turn to carry the torch forward and fulfil the oldest duty of philosophy: awaken people to choose their own way of approaching life.

This book could be labelled as *existentialism for people with baggage*. While existentialists often took it as a self-evident starting point that human beings are 'cast in this world… condemned to be free', as Sartre famously put it,[3] I think that we actually carry quite a lot of baggage that stands in the way of our freedom. Some of this baggage, such as many of our emotional reactions, is a result of evolution – for example, a fear of darkness and dread of abandonment both served our survival in the savannah. Lots of this baggage, though, such as our ideals about what a successful and admirable life looks like, comes from the culture we grew up in. To a large degree, our evolutionary and cultural programming determines how we approach situations, what options we see for ourselves and what things we value.

If we ignore this baggage, we will not be able to liberate ourselves. This is why the emphasis in this book is on *unlearning*. There is a liberated way of living through combining contentment with excitement. But to get there we have to recognize and tackle our baggage. Quoting Master Yoda from *Star Wars*, 'you must unlearn what you have learned'.[4] That's why the first six chapters are about what we should *stop* doing, before we get to what we should *start* doing. Once we break free from following the wrong demands, starting to do the right things will come quite naturally.

This Is Not a Book About Success

What if you sacrificed everything – your time with family and friends, your hobbies, even your health – in order to be successful? And then found out that it was all a hoax: life equipped with all that success does not taste any sweeter. This is a familiar narrative to many. It has its roots in people rushing towards 'success' without stopping to think what 'success' actually means for them.

It is not a compliment to humanity that, if you want your self-help book to succeed, publishers recommend putting 'success' in the title. The majority of self-help book buyers are not actually interested in learning about themselves or about how to be better people. They are interested in success. And by success they mean running faster than the guy next door in a narrowly defined race they did not choose to be part of. Aiming for success – what a waste of a perfectly good life!

The pursuit of success is a syndrome of not knowing what you want out of life. You don't know what is valuable in life or what pursuits are worth the effort. You have found nothing worth fighting for. And, because of that, you settle with the second-best goal: impressing others by doing or having more – better grades, more money, a bigger house or a more expensive watch or dress. This life of one-upmanship is a terrible waste of energy. You were given a unique life to live, but you're throwing it away in empty competing, because you never took the time to think about what you want out of life. It saddens me to see how many people are so busy with accomplishing that they never take the time to think what is *actually worth* accomplishing.

One comic strip that has stuck with me throughout the years depicts two men dragging a heavy load. A third man offers wheels to put under their cart, but they say, 'Sorry, we are too busy…' That's how I sometimes feel teaching my 'Art of Living' course at Aalto University in Helsinki. As it is an elective course, the students taking it tend to be those already on the path to better living. The ones most in need of the course, the ones rushing through life with the narrowest horse blinkers, completely miss out on the lessons of the course. They look at the course description and see that it does not help them to get from A to B. What they don't see is that the course would help them to select better 'B's to aim for. Only when a major life crisis forces them to stop later on will they come to realize the value of learning to re-evaluate such a narrow life direction.

This is not a book with optimized strategies to get from A to B. There are too many *success-help* books out there about that already. Would it not be wiser to first learn to identify which goals are worthwhile for you? Management guru Peter Drucker expressed this well: 'there is surely nothing quite so useless as doing with great efficiency what should not be done at all'.[5] This is not a book about how to improve your efficiency, but about what you should and should not pursue in your life. This book will not teach you about doing things right, but about how to do the right things.

Too few books discuss what the end goals worth striving for in life are – or how to identify the right things to pursue. This latter genre necessitates more introspection, challenging our assumptions and learning to listen to our soul. For the sake of ease (and to distinguish it from 'self-help'), let's call it *self-search*. It guides you in choosing goals worth pursuing, values worth fighting for and attitudes worth having towards life. This genre has a long history – its (Western) roots can be found in ancient Greece and Rome, where philosophers like Socrates, Aristotle, Epicurus, Seneca and Epictetus were the stars of their era, gathering younger and older followers. We could even think of self-search as a sub-genre of self-help, complementing the vast stock of success-help books already on the shelves. *Meditations* by the Roman emperor Marcus Aurelius is a self-help book – quite literally, as it seems to be the life advice that he wrote for himself. My book aims to be part of the same noble tradition of self-searching, but it anchors its advice to the latest findings in behavioural and social sciences.[6]

So, this is a book of science-based self-search, about existentialism for people with baggage, where my under-standing of this baggage is informed by the latest psycho-logical research. Use this book to recalibrate your North Star. Use it to challenge the constraints of your current world view that keep you stuck. Use it to find energizing and valuable goals for your life. *Then* read a book about the best strategies to get there.

The Opportunity to Be Born for a Third Time

Allow me to offer one final way to describe what this book is about. The mission of this book is to aim to offer you a chance to be born for a third time.[7]

The first time is the *physical birth* – when a child emerges from the mother's womb and breathes for the first time. The second time is the *cultural birth* – those first years in which you acquire the language of your caregivers. Simultaneously, you also internalize their values, prejudices, taboos, norms and life goals. In a word, their world view becomes your world view. No longer a helpless baby who merely eats, grows and poops, you become an encultured self, capable of thinking and guiding your behaviour by the world view you acquired from your surroundings. This is the second birth.

The third birth takes the longest and is something people accomplish to varying degrees in their lives. Some never go through this birth. This is the *birth of an individual* – becoming aware of your inner life and values, and having the courage to let them guide your actions.

Immanuel Kant, one of the foundational modern Western philosophers, described this as the 'human being's emergence from his self-incurred minority'.[8] Too easily, we humans subsume our will to the direction of others, lacking resolution and courage to carve our own path. In his groundbreaking 1784 essay 'What is enlightenment?', Kant offered a motto for the enlightenment movement that was then sweeping through Europe: 'have courage to make use of your *own* understanding!'[9] In harsh terms, Kant condemned the 'laziness and cowardice' that had led too many humans to live like 'domesticated animals' afraid to take a single step 'without the walking cart in which they have confined them'. Even highly successful people are nothing but successful domesticated animals if they have not defined their own terms of success, and if they do not follow their own heart. Like lions afraid of the whip, they are just jumping through hoops on someone else's command. Kant's was a battle cry for the freedom of spirit: the ability to use our own reason in all matters, to be in charge of our own life choices and to carve our own path in life.

In the spirit of enlightenment, the goal of this book is to help you to become who you are. You have a mind, but do you have a self? And is that self something you yourself have chosen? I want to help you to build that self; to have more clarity about who you are and what you value. In the words of author Bill Deresiewicz, I want to help you to 'find out not just who you wish to be, but who you are already, underneath what everyone has wanted you to think about yourself'.[10] Deresiewicz notes that everyone is born with a mind, but only through the 'act of introspection, of self-examination, of establishing communication between the mind and the heart, the mind and experience' do you become 'an individual, a unique being – a soul'.[11]

I want to help you step off the treadmill for a second, see the rat race for what it is and see the opportunities that exist outside of it. Taking a moment to breathe outside of your current strivings helps you to figure out 'just what it is that's worth wanting'.[12]

The aims of this book can be summarized in two steps:

- Step 1: Detach yourself from all the unnecessary expectations, fears and pressures to be able to accept life as it is. This is the task of Part I: Kill the Ego and Part II: Kill the Expectations.
- Step 2: Liberated, pursue the things that you most value in life. This will be explored in Part III: Start Living Your Own Life.

In distilling the recipe for good life into those two steps, I have synthesized all the wisdom I have gained over the years about how to approach life, through conducting psychological research in the laboratory, reading the classic wisdom teachers – from Aristotle and Marcus Aurelius to Lao Tzu and Confucius – and, most importantly, by hitchhiking across Finland, attending rock festivals and stumbling upon various larger-than-life characters across the country. You'll learn about the moment of revelation on human connection I had in a basement party full of philosophy students, about what happened when I stumbled into a karaoke bar during a work trip to the remote city of Kajaani and what my grandfather taught me about the years he spent in the trenches during World War II, fighting against the Soviet Union's invasion. I will offer to you the most reliable signposts I have identified to help you steer a steady course towards what good life is for you.

So here we are, at this moment. You arrived here, in the words of Deresiewicz, 'inscribed with all the ways of thinking and feeling that the world has been instilling in you from the moment you were born: the myths, the narratives, the pieties, the assumptions, the values, the sacred words'.[13] While your current world view has taken you to where you are now, parts of it hold you back, forming an invisible cage that limits what you dare to dream about and what choices you have the courage to make.

I want to help you to liberate yourself from those limits, and enable you to identify goals and values that are truly your own – something you wholeheartedly embrace.

But before we can learn what these meaningful things are, we must first clear a few obstacles from our way. Because often the problem is not that we do not know what is valuable in life, but that there are certain deeply ingrained false cultural narratives holding us back. Thus, in the next few chapters, you'll practise the art of unlearning by stopping caring about things you should not care about – others' opinions about you, your past, your future and even your vain pursuit of happiness. Despite their strong grip on you, ultimately they don't matter. You'll need to practise the art of acceptance to make room for the art of excitement. This will lead you towards the excited acceptance of life, where, content with the present, you are energized to pursue a better future for yourself and those around you.

PART I: Kill the Ego

CHAPTER 1

———

STOP CARING ABOUT YOUR OWN HAPPINESS

So you want to be happy? Don't.

I am not saying you shouldn't *be* happy. What I am saying is that you shouldn't *aim* to be happy. There is nothing wrong with being happy when the occasion arises. I have been known to be happy myself. However, happiness is a poor goal for life.

In recent decades, Westerners have become more and more obsessed with happiness. The quest for happiness has become an industry, with annual spending on mental wellness estimated to be at $130 billion.[14] Companies like Amazon, Google and SAP employ Chief Happiness Officers, and the United Arab Emirates even has a Minister of Happiness. Newspapers and YouTube influencers promise 'five tricks to make you happy', while advertisements bombard us with campaigns filled with happy people, telling us to purchase a 'Happy Meal' or to 'Open Happiness!' Even storybooks for small children in Western countries, when compared to East Asian storybooks, contain more excited faces and wider smiles, silently pressuring children to think that they are expected to always be happy.[15]

'Good vibes only' might sound like an innocent slogan, but it is just another way of telling you how you should feel. It pressures you to bury the negative and hide your sadness from others. It is toxic positivity in action.

All of this has led to a situation where being happy has become a cultural norm and a self-evident aim of life.[16] Don't we all want to be happy? Isn't that what we are supposed to strive for in life, more happiness? Happiness has become the holy cow of our age, and we are willing to make many sacrifices to please this smiling idol of worship.

There are certainly many benefits to being happy. Positive emotions broaden our thinking and make our imagination fly.[17] Sharing a laugh or smiling together helps us to connect with other people.[18] Being happy might be good for our health, too.[19] Also – and this almost goes without saying – it feels good to be happy.

But while *being* happy can be a good thing, *pursuing* happiness might actually be bad for us. The tyranny of toxic positivity, that allows no negative feelings, is harmful. As Professor Adam Grant summarized the state of the science: 'There's reason to believe that the quest for happiness might be a recipe for misery.'[20]

Don't be fooled by the false prophets. Don't sacrifice the good things in life in the vain hope of becoming happier – there are detrimental downsides to this. Below, I've outlined four reasons why you should not pursue happiness.

1. You are seeking happiness in the wrong places

When you think about a happy life, what images come to mind? The chances are you start thinking about yachts and champagne, trips to expensive resorts with infinity pools and the kind of polished and carefully curated pictures of luxury you see on Instagram. In other words, you associate expensiveness with happiness.

This is no surprise given that the companies selling those products have spent billions in advertising to associate happiness with material products. They want you to forget that many key sources of happiness don't cost money: for example, hugging a friend you have not seen for a year, going to play in the park with your family or going for a hike in the forest near your home. Doing things you enjoy with people you care about is typically the best way to find happiness – and that does not have to involve much money. The happiest moments are the ones when you are too immersed in the actual experience to remember to take a picture of it.

This is the first problem when it comes to our chase for happiness. The search for happiness leads us to follow a narrow cultural script focusing on materialistic pursuits. We strive for a bigger house, a bigger car, the latest electronic gadgets or a holiday under the palm trees. Professor Jean Twenge, an expert on generational differences, has been alarmed by the ongoing rise of materialism: 'Compared to previous generations, recent high school graduates are more likely to want lots of money and nice things, but less likely to say they're willing to work hard to earn them.'[21]

If you are like those 62 per cent of high-school students who think that it is important to have a lot of money,[22] then I hate to break this to you: you are not heading for happiness with that goal. Many studies have shown that people pursuing the infamous trio of money, fame and good looks as their life goals are less happy than those who have found more valuable goals for their life (more on that later).[23] Money is, of course, a useful tool that can help you achieve many worthy goals in life, and can give you a sense of comfort and security, but making money your life goal is putting the cart before the horse. To get their fingers moving, pianists practise by playing scales. It is repetitive and boring, but necessary to build up the ability to play Beethoven's sonatas and other masterpieces of music. Having money as a goal in life is like having playing scales as your only aim – boring, and missing what makes life beautiful.

2. The attempt to maximize happiness ironically diminishes it

Think about watching a short clip where a popular figure skater wins a gold medal. The crowd goes wild and the skater enthusiastically celebrates with her coach. Would watching the clip make you feel happy? The probable answer is yes, because this kind of film clip triggers positive feelings in people. But here is the twist: before researchers showed this film to an audience, half of the participants were asked to read a short note that stated that 'happiness not only feels good, it also carries important benefits: the happier people can make themselves feel from moment to moment, the more likely they are to be successful, healthy and popular'.[24]

So evil! The researchers in effect made people *value happiness more* to see how this affected their feelings after watching the film. It turned out that it did have an effect: the people who read the statement reported being less happy after watching the film than other people watching the same film. In other words, valuing happiness made them feel less happy. The reason: *they reported being disappointed with their own feelings*. Perhaps the figure skater's joy made them smile a bit, but they would have wanted to derive even more happiness from the film, and this made them frustrated.

This is why the pursuit of happiness is so dangerous. Research shows that people who put a high value on happiness are, on average, less happy than people less concerned with being happy.[25] Victims of our modern obsession with happiness are so eager to optimize their joy that they are unable to settle down and be satisfied with anything. Writer Eric Weiner called such people 'hedonic floaters' as he could see that their 'perpetual pursuit of happiness' makes them unable to fully commit to anything, be it a marriage or a career.[26] They are the kind of people who live in a house for ten years but are unable to call it a home, as they are neurotically flipping through the housing ads for better options. Unfortunately, durable happiness often comes from long-term commitment and the ability to settle down and enjoy the moment – exactly the things that the happiness obsession makes us miss out on.

3. Exclusive focus on your own happiness makes you selfish and lonely

I once saw a man wearing a T-shirt stating, 'I am happy today, so shut up and leave me alone.' It adeptly summarizes what is so damaging about the way we think about happiness – the Western notion of happiness is so self-centred that it easily leads us to focus only on ourselves. Looking out for number one 'begins with the belief that you have a moral right to take actions aimed at giving you the greatest amount of pleasure and least amount of pain', as famously defined by Robert Ringer in his 1977 bestseller *Looking Out for # 1*[27]. The fact that more than two million copies of this motivational book have been sold testifies to the appeal of preaching the gospel of self-interest and the pursuit of the 'greatest amount of happiness' for yourself.[28]

Unfortunately, too much navel-gazing and self-interest backfires. One study found that the more people valued happiness, the lonelier they felt.[29] One reason for this was revealed by another study, which demonstrated that happy people behave more selfishly than sad people.[30] Blinded by an exclusive focus on ourselves and our own happiness, we lose touch with other people. We end up living only for ourselves, as Robert Putnam summarized the modern American condition in his bestselling book *Bowling Alone: The Collapse and Revival of American Community*.[31] Positivity is at its most toxic when we cut out friends who are going through a rough period because they have 'bad vibes'. Sacrificing friendships on the altar of happiness might be the most horrible consequence of our modern obsession.

4. The tyranny of toxic positivity makes inevitable moments of unhappiness intolerable

I have cried in my life. Several times. And, hopefully, so have you; because there have been moments in your life when something sad has happened, and you should have cried. The natural and healthy reaction in those situations is to feel sadness – sometimes sadness so overwhelming that tears just burst out and run down your face.

The belief that you ought to be happy becomes especially problematic when you are unhappy. And, believe it or not, everyone is unhappy at times. No one gets through life without disappointments, without losing loved ones or without trying hard and then failing. By caring about something, you expose yourself to the sadness of losing that something. Sadness is the price to pay for having loved someone, for having dared to pursue your own dreams. Yet, as Alfred Tennyson once so eloquently put it, "Tis better to have loved and lost / Than never to have loved at all.'[32]

Being unhappy is all too human. So, you'd better get comfortable with it. However, if you have been indoctrinated into believing that *everyone should be happy*, those inevitable moments of unhappiness become even harder to bear: not only do you feel sad, you also failed at the grand task of being happy. You are sad *and* a failure. Research shows that many of us feel societal pressures to not be sad – and those who feel such pressures tend to feel more sadness.[33] These pressures are especially strong in Western countries, and contribute to people feeling more

23

depressed, having more negative self-evaluations and ruminating more after a failure.[34]

As I mentioned in the Introduction, in 2018, when newspapers around the globe announced that Finland was the happiest country on earth, Finns themselves reacted by questioning the whole survey.[35] They were not willing to accept the accolade. Being happy was not part of their cultural self-image. Instead, we Finns tend to think of ourselves as an introverted and slightly melancholic bunch of people whose emotional lives resonate with sad tangos and heavy metal – Finland has the most heavy metal bands per capita in the world,[36] while Finnish versions of nostalgic Argentinian tangos, where one longs for lost love, have become a mainstay of our national music scene, being the songs Finns sing together after a few drinks. This, paradoxically, might be one factor going for the Finns. As obsession with happiness is not as strong in Finland as in, say, the US, this ability to accept sad emotions as part of life – and scream them out through heavy metal – could actually make Finns happier.

This is why our modern obsession with happiness is so dangerous. It makes life's inevitable moments of sadness more intolerable. It makes us less capable of dealing with setbacks, frustrations and tragedies – which all have their place in human life.

In the end, happiness is just a feeling – and you shouldn't lose sleep over a feeling.

Happiness Is a Thermometer

I have come to think that the best way to think about happiness is as a sort of thermometer. Finnish winters are cold and dark, with temperatures below freezing for a few months in a row. Thus, keeping houses warm has been vital for survival. A thermometer is a useful tool for that: when it is too low, you know something is wrong. Perhaps someone left the door open, a window is leaking or the fire has died out. The thermometer warns you that something needs fixing, initiating you to start the search for a way to get the temperature back up.

But what you don't do when the thermometer is low is fix the thermometer itself. It's the same with happiness.

Human emotions exist for a reason – they are our body's way of signalling whether things are good or whether something needs attention.[37] (More on emotions in Chapter 3.) Starvation signals that now might be the time to focus on finding food. Sadness highlights that we are losing something dear to us. Excitement tells us that whatever we are doing might be worth doing more of in the future. Emotions give us crucially important information that we should pay attention to. When this signal system is broken, various problems ensue. For example, extremely cheerful people tend to engage in riskier behaviour and be more careless about their health and safety.[38] If you want to climb Mount Everest, too much optimism will likely get you killed. That was the fate of Maurice Wilson, who, in 1934, set out to climb the mountain, sure that his faith would lead him to succeed, and thus not bothering to learn the necessary mountaineering skills. His body was found the following year, far from the top. Feeling happy or optimistic in situations that might call for stress, anxiety or fear is not something to strive for, but a malfunction of our emotional system.

Happiness is a useful tool – when it is low, that signals that there might be something in your life that needs fixing. Something is dragging you down, and the low happiness alerts you to identify the culprit. It is thus a good idea to pay some attention to happiness, as it can give you valuable information about the things that make your life better and the things that make your life worse.

So, use happiness as a tool – as an inbuilt system in your brain that gives you emotional signals about things to avoid and things to seek out. But don't focus on the tool when it is the environment that needs to be changed. When the temperature drops, you don't manifest warmth or suppress the cold. You put on a coat. Happiness is a tool, not a goal.

The Best Things in Life Are Best Achieved Indirectly

So, here's the paradox: those most obsessed with making themselves happy end up lonelier, *less* happy and less capable of handling life's inevitable setbacks. They are constantly disappointed with their own feelings. They *want* to be happy because our culture tells us that we *should* be happy.

In their eagerness to derive the maximum happiness out of every life situation, they have lost their ability to enjoy life as it is.

When we forget that happiness is just a feeling, we can be fooled into starting to worship it as some kind of holy goal for life. But even as a feeling, happiness is a nice thing to have. After all, it feels good. So, if happiness is not achieved directly through an attempt to optimize it, are there some alternative pathways along which we can arrive there?

Economist John Kay wrote a whole book about how many goals in life, business, politics and sports are not achieved with exclusive focus on the goal itself, but rather through focusing on something else.[39] In business, maximizing profits as the sole goal of a company rarely works. Such single-minded focus will likely demotivate employees and alienate customers. A company that genuinely cares about its customers and employees, and is excited to build and deliver something they are proud of, will be the one to make more profit. Paradoxically, maximizing profits is best accomplished indirectly. Think of it this way: there is nothing more uncool than a person desperately trying to be cool, while those blessedly oblivious to how they look in the eyes of others radiate an inimitable aura of chillness. When you *try* to follow the latest trends, you've already lost it.

Many things in life are best achieved indirectly. Happiness is clearly one of these goals. The more you value it, the more desperately you pursue it, the more you obsess over it and the more it eludes you. Psychologist Susan David notes that 'real happiness comes through activities you engage in for their own sake rather than for some extrinsic reason, even when the reason is something as seemingly benevolent as the desire to be happy'.[40] Philosopher John Stuart Mill realized this more than 150 years ago, as testified in his autobiography:

> Those only are happy who have their minds fixed on some object other than their own happiness; on the happiness of others, on the improvement of mankind, even on some art or pursuit, followed not as a means, but as itself an ideal end. Aiming thus at something else, they find happiness by the way.[41]

So if you want to be happy, stop striving for it. The next chapters will help you identify more healthy life goals than an obsession with a thermometer.

CHAPTER 2

———

STOP CARING ABOUT
WHAT OTHERS THINK

During a work trip to Kajaani, a tiny city in the middle of Finland far from everything, I decided to grab a beer at a karaoke bar next to the hotel before heading to bed. I wasn't planning on singing, but you know how these things go. After listening to a few performances, I got into the mood and decided that I might as well sing one classic and melancholic Finnish tango song, 'Satumaa'. The singer is longing for a land far away across the sea, where everything would be good, but that only birds can reach. After my performance (which I would classify as mediocre), a fellow punter wanted to buy me a beer as he found the song so moving. Then he asked what I was going to sing next. I ended up staying there until the wee hours, where we – the ten or so customers – sang songs with a passion that far outreached our abilities. But we applauded and encouraged each other enthusiastically after each performance.

The essence of Finnish culture can be found in a Japanese invention. If you travel to a remote village anywhere in Finland with only one bar and one petrol station, the chances are that the bar will have nothing but a few tables and a karaoke microphone. Despite their reputation for being a bit shy and introverted, Finns are surprisingly willing to sing alone in front of total strangers. Unlike the Japanese variant, where the singing takes place in separate rooms where only your own group gathers, in Finland the singing takes place in a central spot in the bar, where everyone can hear you. And you would be mistaken for thinking that everyone who performs is a great singer. It's a surprisingly liberal 'everything goes' attitude in Finnish karaoke bars. You might hear a semi-pro perform Aerosmith's 'I Don't Want to Miss a Thing' so well that afterwards you'll go and ask them which band they sing in (as I recently did), and then the next performer will sing Amy Winehouse but forget half of the lyrics and most of the melody. The range of talent reaches from 'I can't believe what I am hearing' to 'I can't believe what I am hearing', but nobody cares. Both performances will receive the same level of applause and support from the audience. One of my best friends recently reminded me that 'objectively speaking, you are not a great singer' – but when I sing karaoke, the crowd is always encouraging. Nobody is ashamed of themselves in a Finnish karaoke bar.[42]

Shame is a powerful force. So much beauty is lost in many of our lives when it prevents us from expressing ourselves – through singing, through talking to that interesting person, through opening your mouth or moving your body without being scared. Dance like nobody's watching – that is the world we could achieve without shame.

The trap preventing us from living authentically is built by the expectations of others. Instead of listening to ourselves and asking what we want, we listen to others and make the choices that they want. Instead of following our own dreams, we concentrate on appearances: living a life that *looks* like a dream in photos. Posing replaces living. Looking good in the eyes of others becomes so important that you forget to listen to your heart.

You Were Designed to Obey Others

The expectations of others are unavoidable. Sometimes they are very concrete, like the parents of a classmate who bought him an apartment in central Helsinki. The only catch was that, in order to get it, he had to continue his law studies (which he wanted to abandon for a career in the art world). Often, however, the expectations are more subtle: a nod of approval from your father for making the smart, sensible choice, a brief grimace on the face of your mother when you tell her what your boyfriend does for a living. Another friend from high school had a quite successful career in his thirties, including stints at the European Central Bank and financial consulting in Switzerland, but he felt empty inside. One of his friends booked a therapy session for him and drove him there, not heeding his objections. In a matter of minutes, the therapist saw through my friend, helping him to see how he had a dominant mother who always knew what was best for her children and what values and opinions they should have. And how he consequently had become a perfectionist overachiever who always did what was expected of him, but rarely dared to strive for what he himself wanted. This revelation started a transformation. After detours as a wilderness guide in Lapland and special adviser to a minister, he is now studying to become a watchmaker, having just made his first handmade watch – a job I remember him always speaking of with fondness in high school.

Besides our parents, we soak in expectations from our relatives, friends, neighbours, classmates, colleagues – even random people we meet. Then there is the media. We learn the ideals for how we should dress and behave from movies, TV series, newspaper articles and social media.

Unfortunately, as humans, we have a strong tendency to internalize the expectations of others, and they quickly become our own expectations, having a strong influence on what we strive for in life. Research on human motivation calls this 'internal control'. Basically, there are two types of controlled motivation: external and internal control.[43] In both, you don't do things because you want to, but because you feel like you *have to*.[44]

External control is easy to understand: point a gun at a person, and they usually do whatever you ask them to do. In a less dramatic fashion, it's about the incentives and deterrents other people have come up with to make you behave in certain ways. Money is an attractive incentive, but so is approval and praise. Similarly, speeding tickets and other monetary punishments are effective deterrents. As is social disapproval, ostracism, anger and ridicule. External control is about the carrot and stick that make the donkey go in the right direction.

Internal control is more subtle. It is about you forcing yourself to do certain things and punishing yourself with feelings of guilt and shame if you don't. In internal control you have internalized the social expectations so deeply that you start forcing yourself to behave according to them, without the need for someone else to force you.

Internalizing the social norms has been essential for our survival. The human ability to cooperate is unprecedented in the animal kingdom – a result of selective outrooting of those too aggressive to cooperate and the survival of those most obedient to the tribal norms. Modern evolutionary research tells us that humans have engaged in a process of self-domestication in our recent evolutionary history.[45] We domesticated the wolf, selecting less aggressive and more cooperative individuals, leading to modern dogs. However, only recently did researchers realize that we did the same thing to ourselves: we selected less aggressive and more cooperative humans. Our jaws have weakened, our behaviour has become more docile. In tribes, where individuals who were too dominating or disobedient got ostracized, punished and sometimes even killed by others, those more sensitive to following the norms tended to survive better. To live long enough to have offspring, you either fitted in or were pushed out. That's evolutionary pressure at work.

The problem with controlled motivation is that it does not leave room for the more autonomous motivations that are about following your own interests, values and needs; living the life you want.[46] This is where we'll get to in Part III, but, before that, it is necessary to deal with controlled motivation. Because all too often the inability to live the life you want is not due to a lack of personal interests and goals, but rather that these self-selected goals become crowded out by controlled motivations, especially the internalized expectations of others.

Now, I'm not saying that internalizing the norms is a bad thing in itself. As a parent, I'm constantly working to help my children internalize certain norms: don't hit your brother, clear the table after eating, don't swear in public, read books, and so on. The world is a better place when we teach our children decency, compassion, cooperation and the value of hard work. These are shared values worth internalizing. So, let's continue to teach each other various good norms! Civilized life, good societies and caring communities all depend on each individual internalizing certain norms without which living together would be impossible.

Among the good norms you inherited from your parents and society, however, there are bound to be some bad apples preventing you from living the life you want without serving any good purpose. To separate the wheat from the chaff, you need to go beyond just following everything past generations taught you. The more blindly you internalize norms, the less choice you have in regard to which norms to actually internalize.

Escape Blind Norm-Obedience by Exposing Yourself to Different Norms

We inevitably come to internalize the norms of our childhood environment. What our parents, teachers and friends value become what we ourselves value. As we've seen, many of these are good and worthwhile norms to uphold. But perhaps your parents were intolerant people, teaching you to feel hate and contempt towards certain groups of people. Perhaps their politics, relevant and prevalent in their youth, are now outdated. Part of growing up is realizing your parents are not always right.

Breaking free of the norms and world view you were born into is a crucial task of becoming a fully-grown individual, and ending the self-incurred minority that Kant warned us against. Too many go through life without ever truly expanding their world view.

In my early twenties, I studied computer programming and business at the Helsinki University of Technology while simultaneously undertaking a philosophy degree at the University of Helsinki. Active in student life at both universities, I attended parties, post-lecture trips to the pub and other activities, and soon realized that the norms of these two groups were, in many ways, different.

Who's your favourite actor? This is an innocent enough question and, among the business students, the answers involved Hollywood actors like Brad Pitt or Angelina Jolie. Such a 'mainstream' reply would have been met with contempt among the philosophy students, however, who declared

Toshiro Mifune, a star of Akira Kurosawa's Japanese films in the 1960s, to be the greatest actor of all time. Even more to the point, in the business school's cafeteria, choosing a vegetarian option was met with confusion: 'You are a vegetarian; why?' Among philosophy students, it was the one ordering the meat option who was questioned: 'You still eat meat; why?' What movies and music you were supposed to like, what literature you were supposed to know, what political opinions you were supposed to have… the two student worlds, only a few kilometres away from each other, were worlds apart.

I quickly learned the correct ways to navigate these two social realities. When the two worlds crossed – for example, when I bumped into my philosophy friends when hanging out with my engineering friends or vice versa – I was walking on eggshells. There were two personalities in me, one reserved for each group, and I didn't know how to behave when I needed to express both of them simultaneously.

My personality is much more integrated now – but also more self-selected and autonomous. Exploring both social realities allowed me to integrate the best parts of both worlds into who I am today. Encounters with different groups expanded my understanding of different ways of life, of different values and the value of different choices. By being more conscious of the various available world views, I was better equipped to choose the ways of living that best suited my personality. This would not have been possible had I always lived within one bubble. **We typically only become aware of our own beliefs and values when we encounter someone with different beliefs and values.**

Of course, the differences between two Finnish university campuses only get you so far. Even with their differences, both circles took for granted the things that are often taken for granted in Western, Educated, Industrialized, Rich and Democratic societies – the so-called WEIRD societies – where only the minority of the world's population lives.[47] My own world view has been further expanded by travelling to the areas of the world where people don't watch the same Netflix series as I do, such as backpacking through Central America on my own. Furthermore, I have started to intentionally look for books, TV series and movies originating not from Europe or the US – I've read and watched enough of them already – to learn more about what life looks like in places like Iran, Korea, Argentina or Ethiopia: how do they see the world, what do people there dream about? For example, when the latest Israel–Gaza conflict escalated, I watched a few Palestinian and a few Israeli movies that considerably deepened my understanding of how both sides view the conflict.

So, the next time you are trying to decide what movie or TV series to watch or what book to read next, how about choosing something that does not feed you something you already know, but something that can actually expand your horizon? You will not only learn something new about the world view of the chosen group, but you'll also become more aware of your own current world view. If you want to take this a notch further, do what one friend of mine does and become a couch-surfing host – he hosts people from all over the world in his home, sharing a meal with them and learning more about how they look at the world.

Challenge your world view. Escape the narrow set of norms that childhood instilled in you. Seek out people, art and entertainment that look at the world from different viewpoints. And approach these different viewpoints with humble curiosity: what valuable insights about life could you learn from them? This is the way to become conscious about the things you would stay blind to if you only hung out with people who had the same beliefs as you.

This does not mean that you need to abandon your own world view, but rather that you become conscious about it, after which you can choose what parts of it you want to retain. By doing this, your world view is not blindly inherited. It is chosen.

Untangle Your Self-Esteem

I have a colleague who praises me every time we meet. He tells me how great I am at this and that and how grand some of my recent accomplishments are. While it is nice to hear nice things said about you, I don't get much of an ego boost from such praise. Similar to Finnish people dismissing the accolade of being crowned the happiest people on earth, I usually push such praise to the side, wanting to be done with the formalities to get into the actual conversation. At one point, however, I realized that he says these things because he would like to hear me say similar things about him. He needs such praise much more than I do and, in my inability to see the value of such praise, I have failed to deliver it to him. Nowadays, I make a point to try to return the favour with similar praise about his recent accomplishments. This difference is due to us having different *types* of self-esteem.

Did you think that self-esteem is a personal thing? While there is much talk about the benefits of strong self-esteem and how to build that, the conversation should start with understanding the concept right. Instead of *self*-esteem we should call it *other*-esteem because it is ultimately a monitoring tool to estimate whether *others* like you. In 2000, psychologists Mark Leary and Roy Baumeister made a convincing case that self-esteem is ultimately a 'sociometer' – an internal monitor of the degree to which you expect to be valued by others.[48] As they put it, 'the self-esteem system monitors one's eligibility for lasting, desirable relationships'. We gain self-esteem when we observe that others notice, respect and value us. We lose self-esteem when we note how others ignore, discriminate, disrespect or hate us. From the chain of more subtle and more explicit everyday encounters, we slowly build a generalized sense of our own value in the eyes of others. And that is our self-esteem.

Too much discussion focuses on whether self-esteem is *high* or *low*. At one point, it was thought that high self-esteem *causes* various good things in life like success. Then research showed that the opposite was true.[49] High self-esteem was the *consequence* of many good things in life, while artificially boosting self-esteem did not lead to anything good. It turned out that high self-esteem did not make you more successful. Rather, having success tended to increase your self-esteem. Similar to happiness, self-esteem turned out to be a thermometer you should not try to artificially inflate. 'Self-esteem is optimal when we are not pursuing it,' as researchers Jennifer Crocker and Noah Nuer aptly concluded.[50] Like shoulder pads and mullet haircuts, high self-esteem was big in the 1980s, but all the hype about it feels a bit embarrassing nowadays.

To liberate ourselves from needing constant praise from others, we should focus on another distinction: that between *needy* and *stable* self-esteem – what researchers call contingent and non-contingent self-esteem.[51]

Needy self-esteem is fragile and dependent on constant positive feedback from others. To maintain your sense of self-worth, you need continual validation from others that you are worthy. You need someone saying you are good, you need someone praising what you just did, you need people telling you they love you or that they like you. If your partner takes too long to respond to your 'I love you' text, you start to wonder whether something is wrong. Perhaps they don't love you anymore. Your sense of self-worth is constantly on the line, waiting for validation from the people around you.

At worst, you start boosting your own ego by kicking everybody else down. You exaggerate your own skills and achievements, building a positive illusion and invalidating everyone else's accomplishments. You react to negative feedback with anger, blaming everybody other than you – and thus fail to learn from your mistakes. Such bloated self-esteem built on lying to ourselves is extremely vulnerable, and borders on narcissism. This is not a path you want to go down, as it is harmful for both yourself and especially those around you.

As the name suggests, *stable*, or *non-contingent*, *self-esteem* is less dependent on any single interaction or achievement. Here, we have a deeper sense of being 'worthy of esteem and love'[52] and thus can maintain a healthy sense of self-worth even when failing at a task or receiving negative feedback from others. When we learn to love and accept ourselves, our self-esteem is not dependent on others. Building such stable self-esteem is not easy. Some receive this gift from their parents, being unconditionally loved, and, through that, internalizing the sense that they are worthy. If the love we received from our parents was more conditional, repairing this in adult life typically requires considerable practice in aiming to learn to love ourselves unconditionally. Having someone validate you will greatly help, be that someone a partner, a good friend or a therapist.

Now we are better equipped to understand the difference between me and my colleague. I have relatively stable self-esteem. And if you were to ask my brother and sister, I've always had a bit too much of it – although I am better now at hiding it and appearing humble. Thus, I am relatively immune to external praise. Of course, I like to hear positive things said about me, and some negative feedback might sting. But in most cases neither type of feedback 'gets' to me. I take it as information that can be used to improve my way of doing things. My colleague, on the other hand, has more needy self-esteem. Thus, he constantly seeks positive feedback – and by recognizing this need, he is also much better at giving it to others.

This distinction between stable and needy self-esteem can also be seen in how people react to being on stage. One part of my work is public speaking, ranging from academic presentations to keynote speeches for various companies. In a typical year, I might be on a stage over fifty times, being judged by a number of strangers sitting in the audience. Some people totally fear such a job, finding it nerve-wracking. On the other hand, many who do this kind of job for a living get a huge ego boost from being on stage and receiving positive feedback from the audience. For me, it's quite a neutral experience. I don't get too nervous, but I don't get a huge ego boost either. For those with a more needy self-esteem, receiving the applause of hundreds of people might give them validation, injecting a boost to their self-esteem.

Personally, I mainly attempt to treat any feedback I receive as information. I don't attach my self-esteem to my current performance, but more to what I could become. This focus on the future helps me to take any feedback as more or less useful in my quest to become better in my trade. And focusing on improvement has been shown to eliminate the drops in self-esteem that failing at something usually incurs.[53] Feedback for me is not relevant for my current self-esteem, but for my future abilities. Positive feedback is nice, but has low information value. Negative feed back often contains more information about how to improve my act in the future.

The Land of Little Social Comparison

There's a famous line by the Finnish national poet Eino Leino: 'Kell' onni on, se onnen kätkeköön.'[54] Roughly translated, it means: who has happiness should hide it. The point being: don't brag about your happiness.

The popularity of that saying in Finland stems from the modest national temperament. Overt displays of wealth and success are shunned here. In Helsinki, the capital, you will rarely see fancy or expensive cars on the streets. Even the CEOs and financial sharks tend to drive boring Volvos and Volkswagens rather than anything that would make them stick out.

We humans tend to compare ourselves to others; we measure our success in life by examining whether we are doing better than our classmates and neighbours. Research has indeed demonstrated that these social comparisons matter for well-being: our happiness is not only about how much we have, but how much we have compared to others – the same amount of wealth can make you more or less happy depending on who you compare yourself to.[55] The problem is: who we compare ourselves to tends to change, so that we are always a little behind. Climbing the corporate ladder, you always get to know the people just above you. Moving to a wealthier neighbourhood, you will have wealthier neighbours to compare yourself to.

The more dependent your happiness is on comparisons to others, the more likely you are to be dissatisfied with your current life – especially in the world of social media, where the images of people having more fun than you are bombarding you whenever you open your phone. Similarly, tabloids, movies and TV show you a constant stream of people who are more beautiful than you, who have more stunning homes, holidays and meals than you, and who look happier than you. Even if you consciously know that the pictures are not reality, unconsciously you still can't help but compare your life to theirs – and, as a result, feel that your life falls short. This easily drags you down. You are less satisfied with what you have and the constant race to keep up with the Joneses distracts you from being able to live the life you want.

In Finland and the other Nordic countries, people are more oblivious to those social comparisons and more content – their own happiness is less dependent on how they are doing compared to others.[56] There is also less status anxiety in the Nordics, meaning that people are less interested in seeking high status and less worried about not living up to the cultural standards of success.[57] Less worried about adhering to a rigid, societal definition of success, people in Finland can live a bit more freely – they can worry less about their status and think more about what they themselves want to do in life.

In other words, in the Nordics, people are more able to focus on what makes them happy rather than focusing on looking successful in the eyes of others. The rat race ultimately leaves us no happier. What will, however, leave you happier is focusing your energy on what you actually enjoy doing in life.

I once saw one of the wealthiest men in Finland, who had just been in the news about the hundreds of millions he had recently earned from his latest business deal. He was pushing his toddler in a buggy, running a bit to catch the tram. He could have bought himself an expensive car or hired a driver, but he opted for public transportation.

That's what millionaires look like in Finland – just like everyone else.

It Takes Courage to Be Disliked by Others

'Freedom is being disliked by other people.' This is the controversial conclusion delivered in Ichiro Kishimi and Fumitake Koga's book *The Courage to be Disliked*.[58] Social comparison, status anxiety, needy self-esteem, unhelpful yet internalized norms – these stand in the way of you being able to live the life you want. The less they dominate your life, the more room you have to make the choices that represent the better angles of your mind. Occasionally being disliked is proof that you are exercising your freedom to be you, instead of just being pushed by others. Kishimi and Koga ask, 'if you are not living your life for yourself, then who is going to live it for you?'[59]

How, then, to tackle the strong grip the opinions (or imagined opinions) of others have on you? Awareness is often the first step. The better you know what norms and biases guide your life, the better equipped you are to deal with them. All too often, various internalized norms have an influence on what options you see available in any situation. This is why expanding your world view by engaging with people with alternative views on life is so crucial, as I discussed earlier. Self-awareness can also be gained by stopping and reflecting. When you observe something holding you back or pushing you in a certain direction, stop and try to understand the hidden force behind it. What is the norm stopping you or pushing you? Where does it come from and is it worth being obeyed?

Another important step is to choose carefully whose approval you seek. As social animals, we might not be able to completely detach our self-esteem from feedback from other people. In fact, a certain amount of healthy, constructive feedback is often necessary to help keep us on the right track. For example, a friend of mine is in national politics. Now, that is an occupation where, whatever you decide, you are going to receive harsh critique. And when I say 'harsh critique', I mean anything from well-argued op-eds to caricature memes and death threats. In politics, you have to have a thick skin to survive. However, completely ignoring all negative feedback leaves you in an echo chamber where you become enamoured with your in-group's opinions and lose sight of how to actually serve the citizens. My advice to my politician friend: choose specific people from the opposing side of the political spectrum who you respect despite differences in opinion. Pay attention to their feedback – especially to what they say away from the media, when they can say what they really think. That helps you to see what the relevant counterarguments to your current position are. Then ignore all the other feedback.

Similarly, in ordinary life, it is not wise to protect yourself from all negative feedback. You need feedback to improve and root out harmful behaviour. Just become better at choosing whose feedback matters to you. If you try to please everyone, you end up pleasing no one. Instead, like with my friend, think of the people whose feedback is worthy to be listened to. Find the individuals and communities that share your interests and values – the people who you yourself most respect. Focus on what they think of your life choices, while ignoring the rest. If you let any random person's feedback get under your skin, your self-esteem remains too vulnerable. Be picky.

The third step is easiest to say, but may require years of hard work (or even professional counselling) to make into reality: learn to love yourself. The more you are able to see yourself as a worthy being, the less power any external feedback has to put you down. The more you value yourself, the less you need external validation. This is a theme we will come back to in Chapter 8 when we talk about the importance of self-compassion.

In summary: stop caring about what others think. Liberating yourself from the grip that others have on you will not be easy. The tendency to seek approval from others sits deep in human psychology. For exactly this reason, this is an area worth investing in. The work you put in and the progress you make will become visible in a more liberated way of being. You'll have more room to be you and live the kind of life that suits you. That is worth the fight!

CHAPTER 3

STOP CARING ABOUT HOW YOU FEEL

One of the unsung heroes of the Finnish educational system is the emotional literacy our children get taught in kindergarten. The teachers have posters where faces have various emotional expressions and they ask the children what emotion a particular face might be expressing. Then they ask whether they have felt that emotion, and in what situations they might feel it. The teachers tell stories about stuffed animals encountering various situations and ask the students, 'What do you think? What emotion might Poppy the Bear feel in that situation?' Much of that teaching, however, takes place in action. The teachers will consistently interrogate children about what emotions they and their peers might be experiencing: 'You took that other kid's toy. How do you think they are feeling now?' 'That was a nice hug you gave to your friend. How do you think it made them feel?'

Even more importantly, when a child is angry, crying or happy, the teachers help them recognize their own emotions: 'You seem to be sad!', 'You clench your fists, stamp your foot on the ground and yell. What emotion do you think you are experiencing?' I have been immensely grateful that my three children have been able to learn those fundamental life skills in the hands of teachers who know what they are doing. At the same time, when I heard the teachers talk about the various ways they help these kids to recognize their emotions, I couldn't help but think that I know quite a few adults who desperately need that training.

Strong emotions are, well, strong. They overwhelm you. They carry you away. They make you react before your brain is able to say 'stop'. This can lead to terrible mistakes – we come to say things we never would have wanted to say, we come to do things we afterwards deeply regret. Emotions can also make you react on autopilot – a certain emotion triggers you to respond in a certain way without you even thinking about it.

Because of this, we are sometimes led to avoid emotions altogether. That's not a good idea either. The ideal image of the unemotional, stiff-upper-lip, 'rational' person is a recipe for wrong life choices, a duller life and, often, depression and other mental health problems. The more you try to avoid certain emotions, the more strongly they tend to force themselves to the surface. Stop fighting. Emotions are going to be a part of your life, whether you like it or not. So, it's in your best interest to learn how to live with them.

The art of dealing with emotions involves unlearning the wrong ideas and harmful practices we often use to handle them, and learning how to recognize, gain perspective on and accept them. But, before all that, we need to understand what emotions actually are, and why humans have them.

What Are Emotions?

We all know what emotions are. Giving a precise definition, however, has turned out to be a difficult task, even for researchers. Broadly speaking, emotions are a neurochemical system that makes things feel a certain way. Through that, they make us have a certain attitude towards the given thing, often leading to a physical response. Sadness makes us cry and surprise can make us jump, while joy makes us smile and laugh, for example.

Emotions colour our experience. Imagine a pair of glasses that colours your visual field. Disgusting things would be coloured green, while a person saying something mean to you would immediately be coloured red. When you spot your loved one in a crowd, they would be coloured orange, while your favourite football team losing would make everything look blue. That's generally how emotions work. Emotions arise in response to events that are important to you, their distinct colour highlighting how that event is important to you. Getting something you have long wanted causes joy. Losing something you love causes sadness. Frustration or offence cause anger. Encountering something dangerous elicits fear. All emotions have their distinct colours, thus changing how the world looks to you.

Emotions make the world feel a certain way. They colour-code the world to make it easier for us to navigate it. They create various expectations, making us drawn towards certain things while avoiding others. It is through emotions that we relate to the world.

What is the function of emotions?

Evolution equipped animals with emotions to help them react correctly to various situations. Anger pumps adrenaline and noradrenaline through our body, making us better prepared for a fight.[60] Love makes us more likely to hug, kiss and embrace the targets of our affection. Being happy makes us more open to various ideas and experiences.[61] Disgust makes us avoid certain things – the smells of rotten food and excrement elicit disgust for a reason: avoiding them helps us to not get sick. Similarly, fear makes us avoid dangerous objects like snakes and steep cliffs. Having no fear is a recipe for dying in an accident. No surprise then that basic emotions are quite universal, with humans across the world experiencing them.[62] Even other mammals will experience fear, disgust, sadness and happiness – as any pet owner can testify.

At the end of the day, emotions are information. They are an alarm system that alerts you to relevant factors in your current environment. Roughly speaking, there is a sequence that starts from something happening: you see or hear something, or start to think about something. This *event* is automatically *interpreted* in your mind, giving rise to a specific *emotion*. This emotion prepares your body and mind to approach the event with a certain attitude, often accompanied by physical changes: your heart beats faster or slower, and your muscles tighten or relax. All of this makes you respond to the event in a certain way.

EVENT → INTERPRETATION → EMOTION → RESPONSE

If someone hits you and you immediately hit back, the whole sequence can take place in the blink of an eye, with your conscious mind having no time to intervene. However, if you suddenly feel someone hitting you from the side (event) and you first turn around to see what happened, if you realize it was a person's hand hitting you, you next look at their facial expression to interpret whether it was accidental or intentional (interpretation). Only if you see them looking angry will anger arise (emotion) and you may raise your fists to respond (response). If, instead, the person looks at you with a friendly expression and tells you there was a wasp on your hand that they batted away (different interpretation), you might feel a sense of relief and even gratitude (emotion), leading you to thank the person (response). Same event, different interpretation, different emotion.

Emotions are a relatively automatic system that helps you to approach various situations in life with the right attitude. At best, emotions help us, in the words of Susan David, 'cut through pretences and posturing, working as a kind of internal radar to give us the most accurate and insightful read into what's really going on in a situation'.[63]

For example, you might speak to someone and have a strong gut feeling that something isn't right. You might not be able to put your finger on it, but clearly they are hiding something from you.

Emotions are often right – unless they are wrong

Emotions play a vital function in preparing you to react rightly to various situations. However, there is a catch. Emotions don't arise in response to the situation itself, but, rather, 'emotions arise in response to the *meaning structures* of given situations,' as Professor Nico Frijda highlighted.[64] In colouring the reality, they colour them according to your interpretation of that reality. In a crowded subway, a person yells 'you stink' behind your back and you get angry. Then you realize that the words were aimed at someone else, and your anger subsides. Your anger was not caused by the words themselves, but *your interpretation* of those words being aimed at you.

So, while emotions are often right, they can also misfire. Evolution programmed you to feel certain emotions in certain situations because that tended to increase your chances of survival. But, even more than that, your past experiences have taught you to associate certain situations with certain emotions. Both evolution and your past experience can guide you in the right direction, but, sometimes, your current situation has changed so much from the past that your emotions lead you in the wrong direction.

Once, our five-year-old got a stomach bug after dinner. We had eaten sushi, but no other family member got sick.

Simultaneously, we heard that a few of his kindergarten classmates had a similar bug. So, in all likelihood, the sushi had nothing to do with the illness – our son had picked it up at kindergarten. Still, since that event, he hasn't been able to eat sushi. In fact, the smell of it is so disgusting to him that he can't even sit at the dinner table if the rest of us are eating it. Researchers call this *conditioned taste aversion*, a widely documented event in humans and other mammals.[65] It is very functional in helping animals avoid food that makes them sick – as a reflex, it is a literal lifesaver. However, it can also misfire, as my son's case has shown. You might have a friend who drank too many tequila-and-orange-juice cocktails and threw up afterwards. After that, the mere smell of orange juice made them feel sick for years afterwards. The effect is so strong that no amount of rationalization helps: even if you know very well that it was the tequila and not the orange juice that made you sick, the instinctual reaction of disgust to orange juice remains.

Even more typically, your childhood environment can cause emotional reactions that lead you to make a wrong interpretation about the present situation. You might overreact to someone's words because of past trauma – perhaps your parents belittled your accomplishments, for example. Because of this, even a small criticism from your partner can trigger you to feel that they don't appreciate you. Or perhaps you were badly hurt in a past relationship. That's why feelings of affection trigger fear in you, making you push away from anyone you have feelings for.

Crucially, emotions don't tell us about the reality itself. They are subjective; they tell us about *your interpretation* of that reality. Often your interpretation is accurate – somebody behaves rudely, and you are right to feel anger. But emotions can also misfire, being just echoes of something problematic in your past. Such emotions are harmful for your present situation.

Emotions tell you about your instinctive interpretation. And that interpretation involves two components: the environment and you. Your emotions come to tell a story that reveals something about both.

Now that we know what emotions are, we can learn how to deal with them. This starts with some emotional myth-busting and getting rid of a few harmful beliefs about emotions that keep us stuck.

Myth 1: Some Emotions Are Good, Some Emotions Are Bad

One of the most powerful opening lines can be found in Albert Camus' *The Stranger*:

> Mother died today. Or maybe yesterday, I don't know. I got a telegram from the home: 'Mother deceased. Funeral tomorrow. Faithfully yours.' That doesn't mean anything. Maybe it was yesterday.[66]

What makes that opening so unsettling – and helps to set the character of the protagonist – is the lack of any emotion at the news of his mother's death. Later in the novel, this lack of emotion is used as a testimony against the main character in a trial. Not feeling sadness over such devastating news seems to indicate some deep flaw in his character.

We are misled by our tendency to divide emotions into positive and negative – the 'good' emotions and the 'bad' emotions. This leads us to seek the former and avoid the latter. However, that is not how life works. Every emotion has its time and place. When you lose a loved one, you should feel sadness! In some situations, even anger is an appropriate and wise emotion – it signals to others that they have trampled on something that you care deeply about. Too much joyfulness will lead you into trouble, if the situation calls for more alertness.

We should not think about emotions as good or bad. Rather, we should think about them on a scale of helpful to unhelpful. Susan David calls the conventional view of emotions as good or bad, positive or negative, rigid. It keeps us 'hooked by thoughts, feelings and behaviours that don't serve us'.[67] What we really want is emotional agility, the ability to flexibly deal with whatever emotions we face. Such agility starts with recognizing that every emotion has its place (as anyone who has watched the movie *Inside Out* will know).

So, switch your mindset: there are no good or bad emotions. Only ones that are helpful or unhelpful, depending on the situation at hand.

Myth 2: Negative Emotions Are No Good for You

I was once asked to give a motivational speech at the Finnish Association of Cancer Patients. Knowing that everyone in the audience was dealing with cancer made me think twice about what I should and should not say. I knew that 'just stay positive' would be a horribly inappropriate message. Yet, that's the advice that people with cancer sometimes receive. Struggling with cancer will lead to dark thoughts. And so it should. 'Fuck cancer' is a much more honest campaign than any of those dangerous online 'experts' who claim that cancer can be cured with positive thinking. 'Fuck cancer' as a slogan has spread rapidly in recent years, and for good reason – finally, someone put into words what everybody dealing with cancer was feeling. There are many other situations where feeling negative emotions is completely appropriate.

Intolerance of negative emotions has found a strong foothold in modern Western culture. The tyranny of positivity makes us believe there is something wrong with us if we have negative emotions. We might innocently contribute to this trend by telling our friend to 'just think positively', 'pull yourself together', or similar. While flipping the switch to think positively can sometimes work with minor setbacks, when we are dealing with something bigger, somebody telling us to 'think positively' or trying to put a positive spin on the situation simply makes us feel that they don't understand or care about our pain. Their positive attitude leaves us alone with a pain they don't seem willing to acknowledge.

There are two reasons you should not avoid negative emotions. First, you will have them anyway, whether you want to or not. You will not be able to go through life without facing setbacks, disappointments, losing a loved one or being rejected by someone you care about. Research shows that aiming to feel happy in inappropriate situations – like when confronting a partner who cheated on you – actually makes you feel less happy.[68] This is life – it will inevitably involve both positive and negative emotions. Negative emotions are a sign that you care. Without love there is no sorrow.

Second, quite often, negative emotions are useful and will help you to make the right choices in life. Research has shown that, in appropriate situations, negative emotions can make us less biased and better able to form arguments, be more polite and attentive to others, and even encourage perseverance.[69] All negative emotions have an important function. A healthy dose of anger can help you to stand up for your rights by not allowing people to push you around. Reasonable levels of fear will help you to not take unwanted risks. Negative emotions can signal to you that there is something wrong in your relationship or that you have an asshole of a boss at work. This helps you to think twice about whether there is something that needs to change in regard to your life.

When people tell Susan David that 'I don't want to fail' or 'I don't want to get hurt', she tends to respond that those, unfortunately, are 'dead people's goals'.[70] For those of us who still have a beating heart, negative emotions will be a part of life. Sadness signals that you have found something you care about. It means you have loved something. Discomfort tells you that you have found something meaningful to fight for. Experiencing pain is an unavoidable side effect of being alive.

Life is not about *avoiding* pain, but about *choosing* your pain. A better attitude towards pain starts with asking yourself what things are worth feeling pain for.

Myth 3: If You Have an Unwanted Emotion, Try to Suppress It

As I've already highlighted, instead of avoiding their negative feelings, Finns tend to sing them out. The worst thing you can do with unwanted negative feelings is to try to suppress them. That only reinforces them, while the vain struggle doubles your burden. All feelings are part of life and avoiding negative feelings is like avoiding rainy days.

Bottling up emotions is a dysfunctional way to deal with them. Bottlers try to push the emotion away, avoid thinking about it, never allowing them to come to the surface and get on with things.[71] They might try distracting themselves by doing something else, or zoning out with alcohol or other drugs. Fighters turn against the emotion, arguing with themselves, trying to force themselves to feel something else, or even bullying themselves for feeling the 'wrong' emotion.[72] As a result, both bottlers and fighters miss the message that the emotion is trying to tell them. For example, they remain stuck in a job that makes them unhappy, as they push on, not paying attention to the misery the role is causing them.

In emotional ju-jitsu, the worst move we can make is to try to suppress or fight against an emotion. Within our mind, what we pay attention to grows. And fighting against something keeps our focus on it. Pushing against a strong emotion tends to make that emotion even bigger. In this way, emotions are like martial arts masters who use their opponent's strength against them.

Unfortunately, too many of us are taught to suppress our emotions. The British comedy actor Robert Webb has been outspoken about how all of the 'be a man, stop crying, man up' talk aimed at boys amounts to 'training boys to ignore their feelings'. When boys don't recognize and are not allowed to express their feelings, too much of it comes out as anger: 'I get angry when I am frightened, I get angry when I am embarrassed.' Lacking skills to detect your own emotions and wearing 'a complete lack of self-awareness as a badge of pride' is going to 'leave you unprepared for adversity'.[73]

Boys are told that 'big boys don't cry' and girls are told to keep their feelings to themselves. When the Disney movie *Frozen* became a huge success, I felt that one key attraction of it was Elsa's battle against the mould of being the good girl who never expresses anger or other negative emotions. In the hit song 'Let It Go' she sings about the need to be the good girl who conceals all emotions, hiding everything that doesn't fit the mould. The song marks the moment when Elsa is no longer able to bottle the emotions inside her. Instead, they are displayed in a dramatic way, revealing her magical powers.

Emotions tend to come out, whether we like it or not. And if they have grown within us for too long, they might come out too forcefully, compared to if we had allowed them to surface before they grew too hot to handle. We've all been in a situation where something small irritates us about a loved one, but we try to ignore it. Then, suddenly, we snap at them in a way that is at odds with the actual situation, because we are not just reacting to the situation currently at hand, but a build-up of everything that has happened before that we've ignored and not addressed.

In our twenties, a good friend of mine suffered from depression. His father's advice was to talk about it – with family, with friends. Bottling it up would just make matters worse. So, he told us about it and having it out in the open helped. Instead of forcing a happy face, being honest about his feelings with those who cared about him made the situation easier.

While there are situations that require you to control your emotions, completely suppressing them does not work. You must find outlets for your negative emotions, be it through talking about them with friends or in therapy, singing or dancing them out, painting them on the canvas, writing about them in a journal, sweating them out through jogging in nature or kicking the boxing bag in martial arts training. That way you can start learning to live with them.

How to Hang out with Your Emotions

Ignoring emotions is, to be frank, stupid. As I hope you can now see, they contain vitally important information about your situation. Quite often, they alarm you about subtle cues your conscious mind is not able to detect. So, ignore emotions at your own peril.

Blindly following your emotions is equally unwise. They can misfire, being triggered by some past trauma, by your misinterpretation of the situation or by some evolutionary reaction that does not work in the modern world.

So, what to do?

Step 1: Become aware of your emotions

Living adaptively with emotions starts with becoming aware of them. The less you are aware of your own emotions, the more they control you. We have all seen a five-year-old throwing a tantrum while screaming, 'I am not angry.' They are likely to truly believe so. Their world is so coloured by the emotion that they feel that everything around them is *frustrating*, rather than realizing that they themselves are *frustrated*. The strong emotion has carried them away to such a degree that they lack the perspective to recognize it.

Unfortunately, way too many adults are exactly the same. Overwhelmed by some unrecognized emotion, they come to respond to the world as seen through that emotion. Stressed out, they yell at their friend, partner or child, overreacting to something the other did – even though the true source of irritation is within themselves. Many marriages have unravelled because one party has some unrecognized emotional issues stemming from their past, but falsely come to think that it is their partner who causes these negative feelings.

So, whenever you feel moved by an emotion, ask yourself, what is it that I'm feeling right now? Especially when you feel you are about to be carried away by some strong emotions, pausing to briefly think what feelings you are having is helpful. It opens up the possibility to recognize what that emotion is.

One good way to gain awareness of your emotions is labelling them, just as the kindergarten teachers do with kids in Finland. To label an emotion, that emotion first needs to have a name. While all languages have a word for happiness and sadness, some more complex emotions have only been recognized by certain cultures. Germans have famously contributed *schadenfreude* to the world, the pleasure derived from seeing someone else's misfortune. Finns, in turn, have *morkkis*, the blend of sadness and regret you feel after a night of partying, what the British may call 'the fear'. Morkkis is a sort of emotional hangover. Sometimes, you might have something concrete you did or said to feel morkkis about. But, more often, it is a general sense of regret and shame about the previous night, without being about anything in particular. Now, don't ask me what it says about Finnish and British culture that we both have a phrase for that!

Whether it is anger, nostalgia, jealousy, guilt or morkkis you are feeling, labelling it is a great way of gaining awareness. Stop and think: what is the emotion that I am having? How should I label it? If there is a recurring emotion you are dealing with, you can even give it a nickname. For example, if you are dealing with stage fright whenever you need to give a presentation, you can name it 'the spotlight shivers' or 'the stare scare' to make it feel a bit less intimidating.

My friend and compassion researcher, Miia Paakkanen, told me that when she notices a difficult feeling she tends to sit down with it. She picks up a stuffed animal that represents her as a small child. She hugs that small version of herself and asks: when have you experienced this feeling? Usually, some situations quickly come to her mind. 'When I understand and catch up with that moment in my past life where the feeling was present, the feeling in the present loses its grip.' Getting to the root causes of the present feeling helps her to not get caught up in it, freeing her to choose how to relate to it in the present.

Ultimately, there are two types of emotions: recognized and unrecognized. And the latter control you on autopilot, as you have not acknowledged them and their influence. They colour your experience without you recognizing how your experience has changed. Thus, practising the art of recognizing and labelling your emotions is a crucial first step in gaining freedom from their influence.

Step 2: Gain perspective on your emotions

The second step is to gain some distance from your emotions. Labelling the emotion is a good start. By giving it a name, you can start creating a relationship with it. Instead of it automatically colouring your vision, you start seeing it in action; you start observing how it is *actually* colouring how you see the world.

Remember: you *are not* your emotions. You *have* emotions. A simple technique taught by therapist Russ Harris is to change the way you talk about your emotions.[74] Instead of saying, 'I am angry', say 'I have angry feelings.' Instead of saying, 'I am stressed', say 'I notice I feel stress.' This simple shift in phrasing already reminds you that you are not your emotions but you are just having them. Another similar trick is to talk about yourself in the third person. Instead of 'I am frustrated,' I would say, 'Frank is frustrated.' Again, this builds some distance to the emotion, allowing you to observe it with some perspective. Another trick is to write down what you are feeling. If your mind keeps telling you, 'I am a fraud,' writing it down on a piece of paper and rereading it might help you to gain the necessary distance from the feeling, instead of it repeatedly whispering in your ear.

In observing your emotions, the right attitude is that of curiosity and non-judgementalism. Like a child observing a butterfly, just observe the emotion curiously: what features does it have, how exactly does it make you feel? 'Oh, this is *this kind of emotion*,' is the attitude you should be having. You should not judge the emotion, but allow it to be what it is. Instead of seeing the feeling as 'bad' or 'good', just allow it to be.

Step 3: Accept your emotions like you accept clouds

Fighting against an emotion keeps us focused on it. This, as we've seen, ultimately makes the emotion even stronger, as our mind is completely occupied by it. Instead, think about the emotion as a cloud. You wouldn't fight a cloud, would you? When a cloud arrives and blocks the sun, the colours of the world change. In the same way, the world has a different colour to it while the emotion is there. Like a cloud, the emotion floats into the scenery. But, again, just like a cloud, sooner or later it passes by.

When the emotion comes, see it for what it is: an emotion. Allow it to come, because come it will. Harris notes: 'Don't try to get rid of the sensation or alter it. The goal is to see it as it is, and make peace with it. Focus on the sensation until you drop the struggle with it.'[75]

Your emotions are not you. They are something that is happening to you. As long as you struggle against an emotion, you remain hooked by it. Accepting the emotion for what it is loosens its grip on you. Accepting instead of struggling is generally a wise attitude towards things that have happened.

So, whenever an emotion clouds your vision, say 'Hi' to the emotion, label it, accept it and then move on. Let it go. Be 'one with the wind and sky', as the Disney song suggests.

Moving on with Emotions

The art of dealing with emotions is not about feeling better, but about getting better at feeling.[76] As we've explored, this involves three steps:

1. Recognize them.
2. Gain perspective on them.
3. Accept them.

This awareness and acceptance is the key to living in harmony with your emotions. Approach your own feelings like clouds: observe them coming, observe how they shadow your vision and change how things seem to you – and then observe them floating away.

Of course, all of this is easier said than done. You might know exactly how you should deal with emotions, but, in the heat of the moment, you end up reacting automatically. We all do that. As a researcher, I know all too well how to deal with emotions. In theory. However, when I am tired from too little sleep and a long day at work, and one of my children constantly teases his brother, causing the seventh fight of the evening, I sometimes express my emotions, well, a little too loudly. The irritation and anger lead me to shout before I remember to stop and label and accept them.

Nobody is perfect in the art of dealing with emotions. But the crucial thing is this: we can get better. By practising. Wisdom traditions like Stoicism and Buddhism tend to involve plenty of exercises that aim to help in dealing with emotions. Similarly, in therapeutic schools like Acceptance and Commitment Therapy (ACT), various practices aiming to help you to accept your emotions are a core component. They are good resources if you want to learn more about the art of accepting emotions. Reading this book alone will not transform your ability to deal with them. But regular practice will transform you. Whenever you fail, give thanks for the opportunity to practise, and continue to do the exercises. Do them, and then do them again. That way you are able to increasingly liberate yourself from being stuck with your emotions and being at their mercy, and instead have the room to choose which emotions to follow.

Stephen Covey once wrote that 'between stimulus and response, there is a space. In that space is our power to choose our response. In our response lies our growth and our freedom.'[77] The peculiar thing about us humans is that we have the ability to gain perspective on our emotions. We can observe them and choose whether we follow them. Approach your emotions with curiosity; think about what they are trying to say to you. This makes it possible to live with more intention, less reactively.

In the end, feelings are just feelings. Allow them to come and go. Accept them – and move on.

PART II: Kill the Expectations

CHAPTER 4

——

STOP CARING ABOUT YOUR PAST

A few years ago, international press got excited about Finland's coalition government as it consisted of five political parties and each was led by a woman. Not only were they all women, but four out of five of the party leaders were in their thirties. In a world where most countries are led by grumpy old men in dark suits, women in their thirties was a fresh take on what power can look like.

While this is a good example of Nordic gender equality, another remarkable thing was that several key ministers had come from deprived backgrounds. Sanna Marin was the youngest prime minister in the world when she started in that position in 2019, at the age of thirty-four. Her mother grew up in a children's home, her parents divorced when she was just a few years old and her father struggled with alcoholism. Then her mother fell in love with a woman, and she came to grow up in a poor and working-class rainbow family. She was the first in her family to complete high school, went on to study at university and became an MP when she was twenty-nine. Maria Ohisalo, the minister of interior in Marin's government, also had a father who struggled with alcoholism. She and her mother spent her first birthday at a shelter for victims of domestic violence and, later, after her parents divorced, her mother was sometimes dependent on benefits to help pay the rent.

Marin and Ohisalo had the strength and will to not be determined by their background, but to diligently work their way first to university, then into successful political careers. But they also benefitted from being born in Finland, where they could study in the best universities in the country for free, without their parents' wealth determining what options were open for them. Ohisalo, who also did her PhD on poverty, acknowledges the importance of various public services, such as free kindergarten, in helping children from backgrounds such as hers to succeed in life.

Great things happen when the will and the ability meet the opportunity. One wonders how many great politicians other nations are missing because they don't offer similar opportunities for those coming from impoverished backgrounds. Through highly subsidized kindergartens, free high-quality education and various support services for families, Finland aims to ensure that your background does not determine what you can be in life.

On many accounts, Finland is a pretty good place to be born, and I count myself as one of the lucky ones having been born into a society where youth are supported in many ways. The fact that I dared to take the leap and start studying something as obscure as philosophy at university was much aided by the fact that making that choice did not cost me anything.

Did I deserve to be born in Finland? Can I congratulate myself for the great deeds that our founding fathers did to build Finland into such a success story? Of course not. I was not even born when Finland was crafted into a nation or when my grandfathers fought in the trenches to preserve the independence of this country. Why would I get any credit for that? I should merely be grateful for what they have made feel self-evident for my generation – lack of oppression and hunger, a society where it is safe for kids to play outdoors by themselves and where free high-quality education for all is taken as a given.

Accept Your Background

You are not responsible for your background. You can't be praised or blamed for who your parents were. You had no choice in how much money your family had, what kind of neighbourhood you grew up in or what kind of schools and hobbies were available to you. You didn't choose your skin colour or home country. You were thrown into a certain family and life situation without any personal responsibility for it. So, you should not be ashamed of it, no matter how disadvantaged your background might have been. But you should not be proud of it either – as any privileges you enjoyed were equally undeserved.

People often make a big fuss about their family background, their great ancestors and bloodline, or about the great deeds of their nation. While we can be *grateful* for all of that, making such factors a key part of our self-esteem sounds like compensatory behaviour. Trying to push others down by attaching our self-worth to our family or nation tends to be a symptom of being unable to love ourselves. Whatever privileges you have, don't assume that you deserve them, or that they make you somehow better than others. Acknowledge them and be grateful for them. Then move on.

Sometimes, people can also be seen to carry their misfortunes as a badge of honour that makes them feel special and enables them to expect others to treat them as such.[78] Using our disadvantages to elevate ourselves above others is no better than using our privileges to do the same. Our past should not elevate us above others, but it should not push us below others either.

Whatever disadvantages you have, they are not your fault. It might feel unfair that some people were born with so many more opportunities than you. But there is nothing you can do about it, so better to accept it as a fact of life that you have to work much harder to get where they got by just being lucky enough to be born into the right family. Better also to accept that those others might be blind to their privilege, and thus never see the struggle you had to go through to get where you are. Life is fundamentally unfair – a lottery throwing you to be born into a certain family. We can't change our backgrounds or how unequally luck has been distributed in them. If this injustice bothers you, instead of focusing on the past, the best you can do is work to build a society where the next generations have more equal opportunities.

I am not saying that accepting your position is easy. As a man born into a relatively well-off family where both parents stayed together, alive and mentally healthy throughout my childhood, where I faced no oppression or bullying, and where I got to enjoy high-quality public schools, I am not in a position to preach to anybody that accepting your lot is easy. If you are, say, a woman living in Afghanistan, where the Taliban has banned women from speaking in public or participating in secondary or university education, made it illegal for a woman to look at a man who is not a relation, and forced them to cover their whole body in thick cloth in public, what can I say to you?[79] Facing such hostility and oppression, I have no clue how I would react or how well I could tolerate or accept those vast injustices. Yet, even in such a dire situation, the more able you are to accept the conditions that you can't change, the more you free up energy to focus on those you can influence, to make small adjustments that make your situation more tolerable. Viktor Frankl, writing about his observations as a Jewish prisoner in one of the German concentration camps, noted that there were those rare men 'who walked through the huts comforting others, giving away their last piece of bread'.[80] He saw this as proof that the last of human freedom that can't be taken away from us is the freedom 'to choose one's attitude in any given set of circumstances'. The more dire the circumstances, the harder it is to accept and move on. But the better we are able to do this, the freer we are.

Not caring about your past means acknowledging and making peace with it. It is about making your sense of self-worth less dependent on where you come from and more focused on where you are going. If the conditions of your upbringing were exceptionally good, you can't be proud of that. It is a blessing, but it does not make you any better as a human. If they were exceptionally tough, you can't be blamed for that. It is a curse, but it does not make you any worse as a human. Both are just starting positions, and we are only responsible for what we make of those positions. As psychotherapist Alfred Adler famously put it: 'The important thing is not what one is born with, but what use one makes of that equipment.'[81]

Stoic philosopher Epictetus similarly reminds us that ultimately 'you are an actor in a play that is just the way the producer wants it to be. It is short, if that is his wish, or long, if he wants it long. If he wants you to act the part of a beggar, see that you play it skillfully; and similarly if the part is to be a cripple, or an official, or a private person.'[82] You can't influence whether you were born to the world in 1981, 2001, 1961 or 1821. You did not have a say in whether you were born in Finland, the USA, Indonesia, Egypt, Ghana or the UK – or what family and social class you were born into within those countries. Thus, says Epictetus, 'your job is to put on a splendid performance of the role you have been given'.

We all likely have some privileges and some disadvantages in regard to our background. Some have more of one, others more of the other. Instead of fighting that, you are better off acknowledging and becoming aware of both the privileges and the disadvantages that you have in life. The more realistically you can look at them, the better you can start navigating towards life goals suitable for the situation from which you started. Having unrealistic dreams or thinking you deserve something given your background can make your life a bitter chain of disappointments. Start from where you are – and know from where you start – and make the best possible life out of the cards that have been dealt to you.

Life provides conditions and throws you into both wonderful and horrible situations. But they don't define your value or who you are as a human. At the end of the day, you can do just two things: 1. Become aware of and accept your starting point, and 2. Do as much as you can and want to get where you want to get, while recognizing that how hard or easy it is to get there depends on the starting point you did not choose.

Whatever Horrible Thing You Did in the Past, Accept It

It is one thing to accept parts of your background you are not responsible for, but what about those things you *are* responsible for? What about that time you got angry and did something you forever regret? Or that time your neglect brought shame on the whole family? How should you approach all the misdeeds, shameful acts and situations where you hurt other people?

Simple: accept whatever you have done.

You can't change the past. Denying it will not make it go away. Just accept your flaws, acknowledge the damage you have done and make the necessary apologies. That frees you to focus your energy on altering the future: what do you need to change in yourself or in your environment to ensure that a similar mistake will not happen ever again? Make a pact with yourself to make the necessary changes.

Philosopher Hugh LaFollette admits that, as a teenager, he was a racist: 'I grew up a bigot, living in a land of bigots. I walked, talked, acted, thought and imagined like a bigot.'[83] Growing up in Nashville, Tennessee in the 1950s, everyone around him was a racist and he had no direct acquaintance with Black people, so he knew no other way to think. In fact, he did not even know he was a racist, as he thought that the way he and everyone around him were thinking was just the natural order of things. When did he become morally responsible for his bigotry? Was he responsible for it when he was five? How about when he was fifteen?

In his twenties, cracks started to emerge in his world view. 'I watched and listened as [Black people] challenged their inferior legal and moral status. Their elegant words and courageous deeds clashed with my bigoted habits.'[84] At first, he was able to explain away such clashes, but then he decided he was 'forced to evolve' away from his outdated moral outlook. At that moment, realizing that his past ways of thinking had some deep problems, LaFollette had a choice to make. What he could not alter was the past: whatever racist things he had said or done before that moment were already done. They couldn't be undone. As people don't want to admit that they might be morally flawed, many people choose at such points to double down on their previous position, fighting even harder to uphold and justify their old habits. This rigid attitude prevents you from learning from your misdeeds. LaFollette chose otherwise. He recognized that the past was in the past, but that he could still alter his future. No matter how bigoted he grew up, from that moment onwards, he could update his thinking.

If what you did feels too horrible to accept, even then focus your energy on the future. Redeem the consequences of your bad deeds by committing to doing something equally good in the future. Volunteer to help victims of similar bad situations. Be a support person for people in a similar situation you were in, to help them not make the mistake you did. The weightier the bad act in the past, the weightier commitments you should make to having a positive impact in the future. That will not alter the past. But it will make better the only thing we can make better: the future.

While the past can't be altered, you can alter your attitude to your past. Traumatic events can bring you down, but they can also be triggers for growth more often than we think. Post-traumatic growth has been found to be relatively prevalent among various populations, such as soldiers returning from war zones.[85] While not automatic or easy, if you are able to find some meaning in the event – if it helped you to become a better person or if it started some painful yet positive transformation in you – this helps you to learn to accept what happened and see the silver lining in it. Furthermore, sharing what you went through with others, especially others who have gone through similar trauma, tends to help.[86] Making peace with the past starts with thinking what good that past can bring to your future.

The Past Can Be Rectified Only by Focusing on the Future

This attitude of moral growth is what my favourite philosopher, John Dewey, advocates for. He argues that nobody is 'good' or 'evil'; instead, that there are good and evil tendencies in each of us. The same observation was made by the Nobel Prizewinning Russian author Aleksandr Solzhenitsyn, who spent eight years in Soviet prison camps for criticizing Stalin in a private letter. In Stalin's prison camps, it would be easy to conclude that the guards were evil and the prisoners good. Instead, Solzhenitsyn wrote: 'if only it were all so simple! If only there were evil people somewhere insidiously committing evil deeds, and it were necessary only to separate them from the rest of us and destroy them.'[87] Instead, 'the line separating good and evil passes not through states, nor between classes, nor between political parties either – but right through every human heart – and through all human hearts'. At times, each of us is close to sainthood; at other times 'close to being a devil'. Solzhenitsyn himself is a case in point: praised in the Western world as a fighter for liberty who daringly exposed the horrors of Stalin's regime, he was also a Russian nationalist who praised Putin and urged Russia to expand the borders of the Russian empire by taking back Ukraine.[88] Was Solzhenitsyn a hero or a villain? As all of us, he was both.

If you are unwilling to admit that you are flawed and sometimes make mistakes, then you foreclose the possibility for moral growth. The most monstrous crimes humanity has perpetrated are typically conducted by those who believe they have privileged access to 'right principles' and alone occupy the moral high ground. Instead, accept that sometimes you will do blameworthy things, because this makes it possible for you to become better in the future. That's why John Dewey says that 'the good person is precisely the one who is most conscious of the alternative, and is the most concerned to find openings for the newly forming or growing self'.[89] You are not totally bad, you are not totally good. But you can become better.

Accepting that being flawed is part of the human condition – none of us are perfect – is what we need to do to focus our energy into our future, better self. So, fight the tendency to justify whatever you have done – we easily fall into the habit of coming up with eloquent explanations and justifications even for the most impulsive and unthoughtful acts. Instead, accept that sometimes something you did was the result of bad judgement, selfishness, spiteful vengeance or other unhealthy motivations. Take responsibility for what you did, accept that you are not perfect and then put your energy into making yourself a better person in the future.

Solzhenitsyn reminds us that, even in the best of all hearts, there remains 'an unuprooted small corner of evil' that can start growing, if the owner of that heart focuses their energy on justifying the acts of that corner of evil.[90] On the other hand, 'even within hearts overwhelmed by evil, one small bridgehead of good is retained'. Nurturing and cultivating that can start a transformation. The past is in the past. The future is still in the making. As long as we don't accept that past, we remain stuck in it. Accept what you did, plan redeeming acts if necessary and then move on with your life with a focus on a better future.

———

CHAPTER 5

STOP CARING ABOUT WHAT HAPPENS IN THE WORLD

I was startled awake at 3 a.m. when a battered Fiat pulled up near me. Two men, both wearing black shirts and jeans, stepped out and began walking in my direction. A quick glance around alerted me to the fact that I was alone on the street – there was no one else in sight. I was twenty and travelling solo across Europe on a shoestring budget. At that moment, I was in Granada, Spain – a city that my *Lonely Planet* guidebook warned was notorious for its muggings. When I discovered that all the budget hostels were fully booked, sleeping on the street in front of the railway station with my backpack as a pillow sounded like a good idea – after all, there were a few people already doing the same and I could sleep close to them. Now, however, the others had disappeared, it was the dead of night and the two men were approaching me.

In the few seconds I had before they would reach me, I quickly resolved to accept that they would likely take away my mobile phone, my wallet and perhaps even my whole backpack. I decided that I'd agree with all their requests, as all my worldly possessions were not worth the fight. Accepting all possible material losses seemed better than my life being cut short at such a young age. So, when one of the guys started talking, I was prepared to be cooperative.

To my relief, they turned out to be undercover police officers who wanted to know why I was sleeping on the street. I explained that I had no budget for a hotel room and was waiting for a train that was leaving at 6 a.m. They accepted my explanation but warned me that this was quite a dangerous neighbourhood and suggested that I instead went to a street a few blocks away, where the bars stayed open late, with people on the streets, making it a safer place to hang out at that hour.

Life can thrust us into situations that demand immediate and dramatic acceptance. More typically, though, when we have to digest something dramatic, the practice of acceptance takes place over a longer period of time. In those cases, you have to learn to accept life like an emperor would.

Accept Life like an Emperor

Marcus Aurelius once faced a dilemma that the leaders of our nations faced in 2020: how to guard your citizens during a pandemic. He was the emperor of Rome in 165 CE when the Antonine Plague broke out, wreaking havoc across the Roman Empire, causing up to 2,000 deaths a day in Rome alone and killing millions of people – in some affected places, up to a quarter of the whole population. As the emperor, Marcus Aurelius was supposed to do something to protect his citizens. However, without the benefit of modern medical knowledge, he felt helpless. There was little he could do but watch as the horrible plague raged through his empire, killing several people close to him.

His consolation? Stoicism.

'Be like the rock that the waves keep crashing over. It stands unmoved and the raging of the sea falls still around it,' he writes in his *Meditations*.[91] External things as such are not the problem, 'it's your assessment of them'. Whenever you are distressed by anything happening in the external world, 'the pain is not due to the thing itself but to your own estimate of it'.[92] We must learn to be indifferent to things we can't anyways control. 'Why is it so hard when things go against you? If it's imposed by nature, accept it gladly and stop fighting it.'[93] This is how Marcus Aurelius advised himself and how Stoics have been advising people ever since.

It all starts with the ability to separate two things: external *events* and your *reaction* to those events. The former you can't control. The latter you can. This distinction lies at the heart of Stoicism. Learning to accept the world as it is, to be unmoved by whatever adversities life throws at you, is the ideal that this philosophical school advocates: 'It is we who generate the judgments – inscribing them on ourselves. And we don't have to.'[94]

Closer to our own time, author and spiritual teacher, Michael Singer, articulates this insight as follows: 'One of the most amazing things you will ever realize is that the moment in front of you is not bothering you – you are bothering yourself about the moment in front of you.'[95] Singer, as so many modern writers from Massimo Pigliucci, Mark Manson and Ryan Holiday to Albert Ellis, a key founding figure behind modern cognitive behavioural therapies, is inspired by a philosophical school originating in ancient Greece and peaking in ancient Rome when former slave Epictetus taught the Roman elite – and emperor Marcus Aurelius himself became a practising Stoic. What being a Stoic amounts to, in Marcus Aurelius' words, is 'a resolve to accept whatever happens as necessary and familiar, flowing like water from that same source and spring'.[96]

Stoicism is the art of acceptance – the realization that when something has already happened, it is too late to fight it, so you'd better just accept it as it is. *It is what it is.* That is the kernel of Stoicism.

How Russia Taught Finns to Accept Life as It Is

Icelandic people are famous for their stoic acceptance of life, a trait often attributed to the volcanic nature of their home island. As Icelander Erlingur Erlingsson puts it, 'The stoicism is important to deal with the randomness of nature.'[97] With regular earthquakes and more active volcanoes than almost anywhere else in the world, disasters like the sudden volcanic eruption on the small island of Heimaey in 1973 serve as stark reminders of life's vulnerability. The eruption destroyed 400 homes and forced the 5,000 people on the island to evacuate, reminding Icelanders of the precariousness of life on earth. You better not get too attached to your possessions, as they might be taken away from you at any time. Instead of nervousness, such constant reminders of transience can instil a sense of calmness into people. Having accepted that nothing should be taken for granted, they become more capable of appreciating what they have today.

Finland sits atop a stable continental plate devoid of earthquakes and volcanoes. Instead of geothermal activity, it is geopolitical cracks that are at the heart of the Finnish art of acceptance. Finland, with its 5.5 million inhabitants, shares 1,300 km of border with Russia, which has 143 million inhabitants, nuclear bombs, a corrupted ruling elite and a keen interest to annex its smaller neighbours through military invasion. All this makes this sleeping dragon the most vital existential threat to the nation of Finland. Speaking in Washington DC in 2007, Finland's defence minister at the time, Jyri Häkämies, summarized Finland's main geopolitical risks during the last hundred years: 'Given our geographical location, the three main security challenges for Finland today are Russia, Russia and Russia.'[98] This was years before Russia annexed Crimea in 2014, and before it invaded Ukraine in 2022. Right now, Russia would not only take the top three positions when it comes to Finland's existential threats, but sweep the entire top ten.

A film crew from a major American television network had booked an interview with me for April 2022 as part of their visit to Finland to make an episode about why Finland was so happy. After the Russian invasion of Ukraine, they looked at the map, realized how close to Russia Finland is and cancelled their trip, citing the unstable geopolitical situation. I replied by noting to them that, 'Finland has been next to Russia the whole period of its independence – always fully aware of the threat that the expansive country poses for us. In that spirit, the willingness to defend the country is exceptionally high in Finland, with some 80 per cent of males (me included) serving in the army for six to twelve months. Thus, the manpower and equipment of the Finnish army is surprisingly strong for a country of this size. In that sense, I don't believe the situation will be much different in Finland a month from now or even a year from now. Finland will still be independent, with more or less rhetoric coming from Russia – a situation that has not changed much during the hundred years of independence.'

This is the Finnish reality – living next to a militant dictatorship oppressing its citizens has made many Finns exceptionally willing to defend their country with a stoic attitude, fully aware of the fact that this would mean that many of us could come back in a coffin. Live free or die! That was the reality for my grandparents' generation – both of my grandfathers spent years of their youth on the front with a rifle in their hands, defending the country against Soviet invasion – and that could be the reality for my generation as well. What else can you do, given this situation?

The words of president Juho Kusti Paasikivi are often quoted by Finnish politicians when discussing geopolitical matters: 'Acknowledging the facts is the beginning of all wisdom. Going against the facts is a futile effort and will not lead to a successful outcome.'[99] The context of these words was a radio speech addressing the nation on 6 December 1944, Independence Day, as Finland had just signed a harsh peace treaty with the Soviet Union after three years of fighting. Finland had lost territory and had to pay heavy war reparations to the Soviet Union. This was a bitter price to pay – but, most importantly, Finland had remained independent. Paasikivi stated aloud the unyielding facts of the Finnish situation:[100] 'Finland's foreign policy is dominated by our country's relationship with our large eastern neighbour, the Soviet Union. This is our real foreign policy problem, on which we must find a solution and on which the future of our people depends.' Paasikivi noted that 'we are now, on this 27th anniversary of our independence, in the sixth year of the greatest war in world history, at the bottom of the valley into which events have thrown us. The way up will be difficult.'

The resolution to continue, however, was firm: 'Without effort, we will not get up. We need a firm grip. But every step will take us closer to a freer landscape.' Finnish leaders and Finnish citizens were prepared to put in the effort, because, despite the devastating war, they had been able to keep the most important thing, freedom: 'Independence and sovereignty is a prerequisite without which our people cannot live happily and fulfil their mission.'

Assess the situation and acknowledge the facts. Don't shy away from the harsh reality. Accept it as it is. And then, building on this realistic assessment of the situation, you can start carving your own path towards what you value. This is an attitude that was forced upon Finnish people by the war. And it is an attitude that we all should have towards any adversities in life.

From Theory to Practice: How to Acquire the Serene Sense of Indifference

Accept life we must, but the path to indifference and unconditional acceptance of life as it comes is by no means an easy feat. It requires years of intentional practice. Stoicism was not primarily about books and theories, but a way of living. You became a Stoic not by memorizing its doctrines but by living like a Stoic. Stoics developed various practices and techniques that you can apply to acquire the level of indifference that helps you to cope with even the most severe adversities in life.

You can start the art of acceptance by accepting smaller things – trivial nuisances at your work, for example, or the fact that you will never become a top athlete, rock star, ballet dancer, astronaut or whatever your childhood dream career was. Similarly, with parts of your body or character you have always disliked – accept them as they need to be accepted.

But the real test of the art of acceptance is accepting mortality – looking at your loved ones and thinking that either you die before them, or they die before you. Marcus Aurelius advised us to remind ourselves of this 'natural event' regularly until it no longer scares us, but becomes as trivial a part of the life cycle as grapes turning from unripe to ripened to raisins: 'In short, know this: Human lives are brief and trivial. Yesterday a blob of semen; tomorrow embalming fluid, ash. To pass through this brief life as nature demands. To give it up without complaint. Like an olive that ripens and falls. Praising its mother, thanking the tree it grew on.'[101]

If you want to take your acceptance practice up a notch, Aurelius has you covered: as you kiss your son or daughter good night whisper to yourself, 'They may be dead in the morning.'[102] Accepting our mortality, the cruel fact that you will die and so will each of your loved ones, is often the hardest part of the art of acceptance – but also the most liberating.

I still remember the moment I accepted my own mortality; the fact that one day I will die. I was seventeen and had hitchhiked to our family's summer cabin – a small wooden house on a small island in the Finnish gulf. There I was alone, with no other soul on the island. The sun went down, the shadows grew and the forest around the cabin became pitch-black. We never locked the door when we were on the island. But being alone for the first time, I felt a strong urge to lock it, anxiously listening to the squeaks and snaps coming from the forest. 'There is no rational reason to be afraid,' I kept convincing myself. In order to not give in to fear, I decided to leave the door unlocked – but part of me was in terror. At 2 a.m. I went to bed and tried to sleep. However, my heart started pounding every time I heard even the smallest noise. Was that the sound of steps? Was that the sound of the door opening? Having lain awake like that for a few hours, I decided to figure out what the worst thing that could happen was. At the sound of the next squeak, I imagined a murderer opening the door. With my eyes closed and my back turned towards the bedroom door, I imagined the man sneaking towards me. Now he is there at the bedroom door, now he sees me in the bed, now he takes the last steps to be standing just behind my back, observing me in silence. Now he takes the knife out, now his hand raises for the fatal blow, now he hits my back.

And then, nothing.

Of course, there was nobody in the cabin. But letting my scared imagination run its vision to its logical conclusion, I became liberated from its power. The worst thing that could happen would be the assassin of the night murdering me in my sleep. Then I would die and, after that moment, I would no longer worry about the matter. Somehow accepting this possibility, allowing my scary visions to run to their end, calmed me down. If death was the worst outcome, then so be it. I fell asleep and woke up late in the morning to the sound of the birds, with the forest bathing in sunshine.

Accepting death is a tall order. But realizing it helps you to appreciate and seize the time you have together – cherish the mundane moments you spend with each other as you never know which will be the last. Accepting your mortality makes your remaining days on earth feel more unique, precarious and beautiful.

Besides death, the passage of time means constant transitions. The sun rises and the sun goes down – ending some periods of life and starting new ones. Like your children growing up. There will be a last time they sit on your lap, listening as you read them a bedtime story. There will be a last time when you push them on a swing. Sooner or later, they grow up and leave the nest. Having three children, the youngest of whom just turned eight, I write this with a few tears in my eyes, as I realize that there is no longer a toddler in the house and many cute small-child activities have been replaced with cool schoolkid ones. It feels like just yesterday the youngest ran to hug me when I picked him up from kindergarten. Now, he walks home from school by himself – except on those days when he calls to say that he's going to a friend's place first.

I celebrate the grand steps the kids are taking towards maturity – just this weekend I went to see *Oppenheimer*, a movie about how the first atomic bomb was made, with my eleven-year-old, after which we discussed the complexities of political decision-making during World War II. It's amazing to see him growing up, to be able to have these deep conversations about history with him. But, at the same time, he is no longer the toddler whose daily highlight was to look out for the campus bus, whose driver always honked the horn to greet him, my son waving his hand enthusiastically, being the smallest and the most loyal fan of that small blue bus.

The art of acceptance is hard. And if it does not sometimes bring tears into your eyes, you have not practised it hard enough.

Another technique that Marcus Aurelius offers is to examine whatever is bugging you, and to break it down into its smallest constituent parts, so as to make the whole thing trivial. He gives the example of a song. If you want to be indifferent to the effect that a song might have on you, 'analyse the melody into the notes that form it, and as you hear each one, ask yourself whether you're powerless against *that*'. A single note is just a single note – not much emotional baggage there. He recommends this same strategy for whatever is moving you: 'Look at the individual parts and move from analysis to indifference. Apply this to life as a whole.'[103] If a grand transition is bothering you – losing your job or having to deal with illness, for example – attempt to break its consequences into as small and trivial parts as possible. And then try to accept them one by one instead of swallowing the whole grand truth in one sitting.

In our own times, ACT carries the torch of Stoicism forwards.[104] It is a form of behavioural and cognitive therapy that sees psychological inflexibility – being stuck in some unhealthy patterns of thinking – as a primary obstacle to growth and the ability to pursue one's goals, as well as the source of many mental health problems. What the therapy aims to do is help the client to achieve an openness to experience thoughts, emotions and sensations as they are and without any intention to change them.

There are various techniques to get to this acceptance, such as observing one's negative thought dispassionately or repeating it out loud until only its sound remains. If a certain pattern of thinking keeps repeating itself – 'you are not good enough', 'you don't deserve to be loved' or similar – this thought pattern is labelled and given a name. When observing the thought pattern repeating itself, the person thanks their mind for such an interesting thought, and then moves on. By trying out some of these techniques, you can start your own practice of acceptance.

Stop Reading, Start Practising

In conclusion, the only rational attitude towards whatever happens in the world is to accept it. Small or big issue, delightful or horrifying, it is going to be what it is, no matter what your reaction to it is. So, accept life as it is – because that's how it is.

Easier said than done, though, I know. When Marcus Aurelius wrote his *Meditations*, it was originally written for an audience of one: himself. He was not perfect in what he was preaching. And exactly because of that, he wrote advice to himself, to strengthen his resolve, to better his art of acceptance.

What you need to do is to work on your acceptance skills. Acceptance is not just something you have or don't have; it's an attitude that can be improved through training. So, in addition to your bodily workout, make sure your daily practice includes some exercise in the art of acceptance. That way you will be prepared when the shit hits the fan.

CHAPTER 6

STOP CARING ABOUT
YOUR FUTURE SUCCESS

Ville Juurikkala is a Finnish photographer, famous for his portraits of rock stars like Slash, Steven Tyler of Aerosmith and Chester Bennington of Linkin Park.[105] He got a taste of success at a young age, spending his late twenties living in the Hollywood Hills and flying across the world to document tours and shoot music videos for various rock bands. Yet he felt depressed and used alcohol and drugs to escape. 'In LA everything feels like a stage scene. There is a horrible pressure to succeed. After succeeding, you have to succeed again.'[106] Realizing he had to get out before the city killed him, he left his earthly possessions behind and went on a pilgrimage along the famous Camino de Santiago route in Spain. His backpack, camera and wallet got stolen along the way, and, in the following weeks, he walked on without any money, depending on the goodwill of people for a meal and a place to sleep at night. This experience of not possessing anything made him realize how empty success did not make him happy. Instead, 'happiness is not dependent on external things but whether your mind is stuck or letting go'.[107] Having nothing, he had nothing to lose, and this was liberating, allowing him to enjoy the present rather than be afraid about whether he was able to remain successful in the future. He continues to photograph rock bands – but on his own terms, rather than out of a desperate need to succeed.

Iikka Kokko is a Finnish child prodigy.[108] He completed high school in a year, graduating at the age of sixteen, while also studying a year's worth of university-level courses in mathematics. Usually, students in Finland, myself included, *start* their three-year high school at sixteen. To accomplish this, while also working at a pharmacy, he tended to pull twelve-hour-long days. Mathematics fascinates him – 'when you get far enough in mathematics, you can create and play with worlds that would not be real in our world,' he says – and he wants to pursue a career in theoretical astrophysics. He has the talent and he has the discipline. What does the promising young man want to accomplish in his career? 'In forty years, I am fairly satisfied with my life if I have done the career of an average researcher. That's enough for me.'[109]

Iikka seems to love the activity, not success itself. This healthy attitude is often forgotten when love of success overwhelms the love of exploring, the love of learning and the love of engaging in an activity and mastering it. It is nice to accomplish things, and the feeling of getting something great done is, well, great! But success for the sake of success is a recipe for an empty life. A desperate push for success is typically a symptom of the 'I'll be worthy when' syndrome, where lack of self-love and self-esteem deludes a person to chase some external yardsticks they believe will restore their sense of self-worth. But it does not work. If you don't love yourself now, you will not love yourself in a Lamborghini. So, fix that first. Then you can choose whether you would rather smile in a Volvo or a Ferrari.

I am not saying that you should aim to be unsuccessful. When done right, you can set yourself grand goals and aim to accomplish great things. You can often even become more successful than your narrowly success-oriented colleague. But to avoid putting the cart before the horse, it's time to rethink your relationship with success.

Focus on the Process, Not the Outcome

In poker, you have to keep your nerves in a tight situation. Like when Ilari Tahkokallio was playing a major tournament in Berlin. In the middle of a game, a sudden explosion of screaming and panic started to spread from one corner of the room, with people rushing towards the exit, knocking over poker tables on the way. An armed robbery was taking place in the next room, where the cash for the tournament was stored. The robbers got away and, after a few hours of confusion, it was decided that the tournament could continue.

The players came back to the table and used video recordings to check they had the right number of poker chips. Miraculously, the cards from the interrupted round were still on Ilari's table seemingly intact. Ilari had an ace and a ten in his hand, the opponent had an ace and a queen. The tournament referee said that, given the interruption caused by the robbery, the hand would be killed and they would continue with a new draw. However, the other player protested: he had the better hand and had put in all his chips. Winning this hand could make or break his tournament. The referee looked at Ilari and asked, 'What should we do?'

Ilari faced a choice: the odds were strongly against him. He would win the hand if the last revealed card was a ten. Anything else and he would lose. He only had a one in thirteen chance of winning. Afterwards, when Ilari discussed the situation with other players, many colleagues said they would not have continued, as the odds were so clearly against him. The robbery gave him an opportunity to get out of a tight spot, and he should seize it. However, his Finnish colleagues all said that they probably would have continued, to honour the spirit of the game. That's what Ilari also did. He lost the hand, but continued well in the tournament, eventually coming second, and returning home with a €600,000 reward.

So, do you want to be good at poker? If you do, you'd better learn to love the process, not the outcome. The former you can control, the latter you can't. Poker is a game of odds. In any given game, you have a few cards in your hand when the dealer is about to turn over the last card. If you are good at maths, you might be able to calculate that you have, let's say, an 86 per cent chance of winning. Time to put in some money. But be careful – no matter how good your hand, there is still that 14 per cent chance that you lose all the money you put in.

I've spoken with Ilari and a few other professional poker players about how they approach the game. Poker is a game of small margins. Even good players have days when the odds seem to be against them. They make all the right choices, but still keep losing money. Sometimes, bad luck can follow you for weeks or even months, but you have to keep trusting the system, even if it means losing thousands of euros each night; as long as you are making the right choices, you should win in the long run. So, analyse your game, make corrections if you find something wrong with your strategy – and keep playing.

On each individual night, the process and outcome are quite separate. You might have made many well-thought-out moves, but if luck was against you in that big bet you might come home with €10,000 less in cash. On another night, you might make a few fatal mistakes – but because luck was on your side, you bring home €20,000 more than you left with. If you want to stay in the business and keep improving your craft, you should not make the mistake of evaluating your gameplay based on the outcomes. Sometimes you make the right choice and lose; sometimes you make a mistake but still win.

To survive in poker as a professional, to learn and grow (and to be able to sleep peacefully through the night), you simply need to focus on the process, not the outcomes.

This applies to life in general. No matter the area, the outcomes are something you can never fully control. Luck plays a bigger role in our lives than we are usually willing to admit. In business, I have learned to respect those CEOs who openly admit that they have been lucky. Those not acknowledging the impact luck has had tend to have inflated egos that get bigger with each win, until they reach a sense of invincibility – and the inevitable crash-and-burn happens. As I recently wrote in the *Harvard Business Review*, such humble leaders are able to 'put the good of the company above their own egos' and ultimately build stronger and more innovative businesses.[110] While we modern people sometimes live in the hubris of believing everything is in our own hands, most cultures have had a way of reminding themselves of the role of luck in life. The Ancient Stoics used to say, after expressing a goal, 'if fate will have it'. Such as, 'We will sail to Athens, if fate will have it.' Christians have used *Deo Volente*, meaning 'God willing', to similarly emphasize that the fate of any project is partly in the hands of higher powers. Muslims have *inshallah*, also meaning 'if God wills'. Each serves to remind us that the fate of our life is ultimately not in our hands.

When I turned thirty, I decided to create a bucket list of things to do before I die (if fate will have it), which can still be found online.[111] I had a few classic accomplishments on there, such as running a marathon (done) and crossing an ocean on a sailboat (still to do). But when I thought about my career, I couldn't find any milestones that were motivating enough to make the list. This is how I realized that I did not do my job to get a specific title or award or recognition.

I realized that the best things about being a researcher were being able to write for a living – because I enjoy nothing more than a few hours of writing in some café every morning – and being part of a community where you can discuss the things you are excited about with the brightest minds on earth. If I would be able to do those things, I would be happy, no matter the title on my business card. So, my professional bucket list came to include items related to being part of the research community: 'have at least five professor-level contacts whom I can call day or night if an exciting idea hits me' (done) and 'be among the persons that a future philosopher thanks in the acknowledgement section of her or his breakthrough book' (still to do). Then I had items related to writing: 'write a book in academic philosophy' (still to do) and 'write a book about living well for a more general audience' (doing it now). While I've had increasingly good outcomes in my research career, it's the process itself I am in love with.

Similarly, when I have been lecturing my courses about good life and happiness to students at Aalto University here in Finland, I've often asked the students to write a brief reflection about their dreams and aims in life. What has struck me is how ordinary most young people's wishes are. This is an elite institution – the most selective management school in the country – with the alumni occupying top positions in the largest companies of the country. Yet most students don't have grand wishes for success, but rather want to have the ordinary things: a job they find interesting and challenging enough, being able to afford a house, finding a spouse and building a family – with or without the golden retriever. Don't get me wrong, the same students are also ambitious, many getting hired by McKinsey, Accenture or other global consultancies – if they don't end up venturing into having their own start-ups (several unicorn founders are our alumni). Most have the skills and are willing to put in the effort to succeed. But their good life is not tied to their career ambitions. How high or low they are able to climb the career ladder is not what defines their self-worth. Already at a young age, they have realized that a good and meaningful life is more than your pay cheque and title. In this, they epitomize the healthy Finnish attitude to a career that will not diminish your chances of succeeding, but will make you more resilient during the moments when not everything is going according to plan.

So, this is the first lesson in how to relate to your success: learn to focus on the process, not the outcome.

How fear of failure stands in the way of winning

In the 2018 FIFA World Cup, England's team made it to the semi-finals – their best performance in twenty-eight years. More astonishingly, the team overcame the penalty shootout curse that had haunted the national team for generations by beating Colombia in the first knock-out round. That spot of extreme pressure had proved to be nerve-wracking for even the best English players, with the team having lost all the previous World Cup penalty shootouts it had been involved in. There was a new-found psychological strength and playfulness in England's team that had been absent from previous generations. I remember seeing an image of Harry Maguire, Jordan Pickford and other stars of the team riding inflatable unicorns in a pool during the games.[112] At that point, I knew something fundamental had changed in the team psyche. You could never imagine Paul Gascoigne's generation riding inflatable unicorns during a major tournament. 'Excited, not nervous' was the team's attitude now – while previously it had been the opposite, with detrimental consequences during the moments when it mattered the most. Along with the manager, Gareth Southgate, a key person behind this change was Dr Pippa Grange, the team psychologist.

Fear often stands in the way of success in competitive sports. You are so afraid of losing, so afraid of missing that penalty when the whole nation is watching, that you lose your confidence – and end up failing. The past generations of professional English football players were serious guys. And by 'serious' I mean seriously detached from their emotions due to the 'boys don't cry' culture, and thus unable to cope with their emotions when the pressure was at its highest.

Pippa Grange has made her career helping top athletes and other people fear less – and, through that, win more. She describes two different ways of winning: *winning shallow* and *winning deep*. The first is driven by fear. Pippa gives as an example an elite football player she calls 'Paul' to protect his identity, who achieved all his childhood dreams during his career, even getting to lift the trophy he had seen being lifted by his favourite team as a small kid.[113] 'Everyone was cracking beers and carrying on, all smiles and singing,

I joined in but all I felt was empty.' He had lost the joy of playing, the sparkle, through the fear-mongering culture of his club, where the focus was always on *not losing* and where the coach's first comment after his hip injury had been, 'plenty of young talent after your shirt, lad, and they're all better than you'.

In winning deep, your prowess is not motivated by the fear of failure, but is rather about 'expansion and experience and connection' – you are leaving your best self on the pitch. Here, there isn't as desperate a *need* to win, but nevertheless the *feel* of winning is more intense and joyful. Here, success has nothing to do with your worth as a person, but is a positive experience of conquering something grand. Pippa gives the example of Andy Ruiz Jr. who knocked reigning champion Anthony Joshua out in the seventh round of a heavyweight boxing championship match in 2019. He was the clear underdog and could not believe what he accomplished: 'I'm still pinching myself to see if this is true… This is what I've been working for my whole life.'[114]

You put in the effort – in the case of top athletes, an extreme amount of effort – to increase your probabilities to succeed. But the result is never up to you. Not in sports, nor in any other field in life. All you can do is do your best – focus on optimizing the process, and the results may or may not come. 'Results are just the outcome, they are not your worth,' as Pippa puts it.[115]

This same attitude can be found among Finnish elite sportswomen. Wilma Murto is the European champion in pole vaulting and a World Championship bronze medallist.

When asked about her aspirations, she stated that she does not believe that only gold is relevant and everything else is a terrible disappointment. 'For me, the best thing in sports is that every day brings a new opportunity and now it has brought me a realistic chance to aim for the World Championship gold.'[116] Before being able to compete for a place on the podium, however, she had several rough years. She was a teenage sensation, who broke the under-twenty world record in pole vaulting at the age of seventeen, by jumping 471 cm in 2016. However, the following years were gloomy as her performance fell and it took five years before she was able to jump as high again. An outcome-oriented sportsperson would have found such years of mediocre performance intolerable. But Murto was focused on the process: 'The driving force back then was the inner drive, the passion and the belief in my own abilities, that somehow I'll get out of here.'[117] Now, with a few medals in her pocket and her best years ahead of her, she is more confident than ever in her abilities. Grateful for where the process has brought her, she can focus on her performance at the track and field stadium, without being distracted by the gold pressure. Paradoxically, in a sport where you soar close to five metres above the ground and then roll over a bar in a delicate movement with a few centimetres' margin, being totally focused on the process is the only way to actually outperform oneself and win that gold medal.

That's the paradox: focusing on the process tends to produce better outcomes than a direct focus on those outcomes. By caring less about the outcomes while giving your full attention to improving the process, you will outcompete your outcome-obsessed colleague. Life isn't fair: those who learn to want less tend to get more. Not by doing less – they might be equally obsessed with the task itself, be that work, sports, art or something else. But their focus, their obsession and their practice are on the process, rather than the outcome.

When your focus is on avoiding losing, you can only win shallow. When you are excited about improving the process, you set the stage for winning deep.

What's more, through a focus on the process, you will have more fun on the way. A strict outcome focus makes all the steps towards that outcome into a chain of endless duties. All the hours spent on the topic have value only to the degree that they bring forth the desired outcome. If you reach that outcome, you have still lost all the hours spent there because, during those hours, you merely performed chores. And if you don't reach the outcome, then all those hours of struggle will have been fully wasted.

Not so for those focused on the process. For them, life is happening during the practice. The hours spent doing the thing bring joy and value to their life, no matter the outcome. The eventual outcomes are the cherry on top, but the real value of the activities are realized *during* the activities rather than *after* them.

So, want to live more? Want to make your hours and activities count? Learn to love the process, allowing the mercy of good fortune to determine the outcome!

Success Is a Trap

You might have obsessively sought success for years, and then it happens – you finally made it. This might be the worst thing that could happen to you!

As a schoolboy, I was very good at maths. I got top grades in every test in elementary school. My worst score during my first nine years of schooling was twenty-two out of twenty-four in the fourth grade – I had calculated the answers right but had forgotten to put the 'cm' sign after the answer in four cases, and the teacher took off half a point for each. In every other test throughout those years, I either got full marks or one point off full marks. In high school, I continued to excel in maths. Then, in my second year of high school, for the first time I didn't get a top mark. My first reaction: an immediate sense of relief. I felt no disappointment, no frustration for having failed to keep the good numbers rolling; I was just relieved.

My success in maths had become a burden. I desperately needed to succeed, to keep up the standards I had built for myself and to be worthy of the praise teachers were always giving me. Now I was liberated from that.

This did not lower my performance. I still got high grades for the rest of my high-school courses. In the national test at the end of high school, I got fifty-eight out of sixty, placing me in the top 1 per cent nationally. But after that one mishap, I was much less stressed about the exams. I did my best, but I was no longer worried about failing. I concentrated on the process rather than the outcome.

That made maths more fun, and less stressful. For me, it was maths; for someone else it might be English, history, football, playing the piano, drawing, or whatever they happen to be especially good at.

Success can become a trap. You get such good results that you start to expect them in the future. Even worse, everyone around you starts to expect constant success from you too. Your parents talk about how smart you are and boast about your school grades, hobbies or top job to relatives, friends and anyone who listens. Your teacher or boss highlights your good performance in front of others.

All that is, of course, nice, and can boost your self-esteem. But it is also a trap. It makes you afraid of failing. You start to make choices that ensure you retain your successful image. You don't want to disappoint the people in your life who praise your success, so you desperately need to ace that next test as well or go for that next promotion. Not because you enjoy doing what you are doing, but to keep up the image others have of you. In other words, being successful pushes you to become more success-oriented and less process-oriented. Unfortunately, this is detrimental not only for your well-being, but also for your future chance of succeeding. Optimal learning requires you to push yourself to the limit, to take up challenges that are hard enough to make success uncertain. Pushing yourself to the limit is best for your long-term success, but opens you up to short-term failures. If you need to succeed now, you play it safe and do only the things you are certain you can succeed in, and you learn less.

No matter the external praise you receive, keep your eyes on the process. Remember that all this praising unwittingly seduces you to abandon the process focus, turning you into a narrowly success-oriented achiever who no longer loves the activity or the sense of learning and growth that putting in the effort offers.

You Don't Deserve Your Success

'Each man is the architect of his own fortune.' You may have heard this slogan. Perhaps some self-made man has boldly used it to justify their success. It is a widely used saying across the world, having its origins in Ancient Rome: *Faber est suae quisque fortunae.*

Too bad that it is wrong.

Appius Claudius Caecus, a Roman statesman living in roughly 350–250 BCE, used the phrase in a famous speech, and it became a catchphrase in the Roman Empire.[118] It's quite telling that the person coining the phrase was from a privileged upper-class family, who had a wide number of slaves taking care of the household. When you have enslaved others to support your success, it is easy to find the time to come up with self-justifying platitudes about being a 'self-made' man.

Let me get this straight: nobody is alone deserving of their success.

If you were raised by wolves, without any human contact for the first eighteen years of your life; if nobody taught you how to speak or think and you invented such things by yourself; if you never had the protection that a stable state with a military and police force that is on your side provides; if all of these conditions apply to you but you are still successful – then I salute you as the first self-made human in history. In all the other cases, you are merely standing on the shoulders of giants, pushed there by the people who supported you: the upbringing, life advice, values, care, and whatever else your caregivers brought to you when you were a child; the teachers you had and the education you received; the opportunities for play and hobbies you had instead of having to work to support your family – all of these made you who you are, and all of that you received without your own merit, being more or less lucky in the lottery of life conditions.

There is a short video clip I often show to students to demonstrate this phenomenon.[119] A college teacher puts around a hundred students on a starting line of a racetrack and promises that the winner of the race will win $100. Everyone gets ready to run. But, before the competition starts, he gives a few extra instructions:

'Take two steps forward if your parents are still married.'

'Take two steps forward if you had access to private education.'

'Take two steps forward if you never had to help your mum or dad with the bills.'

'Take two steps forward if you never had to wonder where your next meal was going to come from.'

And so forth.

Suddenly, the students are scattered, with some almost halfway to the goal while others are still standing on the starting line. Now, the teacher reminds them that 'every statement I have made has nothing to do with anything any one of you has done, or any decisions you have made'. Yet, some are given a huge head start.

While feeling wildly unfair on a sporting track, this is the reality of life. If your parents were healthy, alive and together during your childhood, if they did not suffer from alcoholism or mental disorders, if there was constantly food on the table, if your neighbourhood was safe and the schools good – then you have been given a head start.

Of course, all of this does not take away from the fact that your own work matters: among those starting in roughly the same area, the faster ones will outcompete the slower ones – so, the one with the most privileges does not automatically win. Also, the most athletic among those starting at the back can improve their position tremendously by passing by the tens of slower ones before the finishing line. Still, they have no realistic chance at winning, as even the half-athletic ones at the front start so much further ahead of them that they will not be able to fully close the gap during the race.

As we touched on in Chapter 4, that is, unfortunately, how life works. We all start with some privileges and some disadvantages. Some have more of one, some way too much of the other. But remember this: it was pure luck that you landed in the starting position you were given. Be grateful for the advantages and try to accept the disadvantages. But don't ever think you deserved them. It was Lady Fortuna at play.

So, then, both your own effort and your starting point determine what you can reach. That is an undeniable fact of life. Don't believe those who say: 'you can be anything you want to be'. These prophets of empty promises leave most people disappointed with life. Their message is especially harsh for those starting with the most disadvantages. What they are saying, in essence, is that their poor starting point is their own fault, that life outcomes are solely the responsibility of the individual in question, not their situation. No wonder it is often those most blind to their own privilege, like Appius Caecus, who make such statements.

But don't believe those who say that 'there is nothing you can do, as your starting point determines everything', either. That is equally untrue. Some people are more ready to seize the few opportunities given to them and, through systematic work, can work their way up from their starting point. If born in a country where education and resources are accessible, they can even become ministers. So, no matter your starting point, there are always some goals you can reach, some improvements you can strive for. Whether you get where you aim, you can never know. But by putting in the effort, you can increase the odds.

My own version of the saying would be: **each person is the striker of their own fortune**. Let me explain. As a striker in a football team, you have to put in your own effort to succeed. Nobody is going to make those goals for you. You have to outsmart the defenders, connect with your teammates and be in the right spot at the right time to make that game-winning shot. Simultaneously, you are not going to make a single goal alone. It is your teammates who set up the attacks and pass the ball to you at the right moment. Without the team and the support it provides, you have zero chance of scoring.

So put in the effort, go all in. But push as you may, always remember to be grateful for those who enabled your success. It was not you alone. It was also pure luck and a plethora of people who supported you in bigger or smaller ways. If you succeed, don't think you deserve it. Instead, be grateful for it.

Some Have Happiness, Everyone Has Summer

There is a beloved Finnish expression that has been handed down for generations: *Onni yksillä, kesä kaikilla*. It translates into 'some have happiness, everyone has summer'.

It is used to remind each other that, while there are aspects of our lives we can influence or change, there are so many things we simply can't control. So, there is no point in envying those who are happy right now, even if we are struggling. Sometimes life gives, sometimes it takes. Tomorrow someone else might be the one having a rough time, while something delightful might come your way.

No matter what our personal situation is, or how much luck and success we have had in our endeavours, ultimately, we are all in the same boat. In Finland, the long, dark winter hits both rich and poor, both the successful and the unsuccessful – everyone has to endure. Equally reliably, after the winter there will be spring that warms bodies and hearts and awakens nature to bloom.

Nature teaches us a lesson here: no matter what your situation is, you can always count on one thing... sooner or later, summer will come to us all.

INTERMISSION

CHAPTER 7

THE CENTRE OF INDIFFERENCE

On Saturday evenings, when the rest of the family has already been asleep for a few hours and I am alone downstairs, I end up watching a two-minute video clip featuring Jim Carrey on the red carpet of the 2017 *Harper's Bazaar* New York Fashion Week 'Icons' party embarrassingly often.[120] The interviewer, Catt Sadler, catches the movie star and asks him what he is doing there. Her facial expression is priceless when Jim Carrey replies: 'There is no meaning to any of this, so I wanted to find the most meaningless thing I could come to – and here I am.'

Sadler reminds Jim that, this year, Fashion Week is celebrating icons.

'Celebrating icons? That is just the absolute lowest-aiming possibility we could come up with!'

'You don't believe that certain icons have the power to make change, to think differently, to be bold, to inspire others? You are one of them!'

'I don't believe in icons, I don't believe in personalities. I believe that peace lies beyond personality... I don't believe you exist... I believe we are a field of energy dancing for itself.'

Catt Sadler has one more go at putting the situation back on track: 'But Jim, you got really dressed up for the occasion, you look good!'

'I did not get dressed up. There is no me. There's just things happening. There are clusters of tetrahedrons moving around together... We don't matter, that is the good news!'

Maybe it is just me, but I find that clip profoundly hilarious. Walking into a Fashion Week event of all places, and reminding humankind that, at the end of the day, none of this actually matters – that we are just piles of atoms moving around according to the blind forces of nature. From the cosmic perspective, what difference does it make what one species of non-furry monkeys does on the third planet of a mid-sized star, when there are millions of other stars with millions of other planets in the universe? Earth existed for 4.5 billion years before humans, and will exist some 5 billion years after we have disappeared, so why cry over the lost opportunities of 1 out of 8 billion humans currently alive? It's like crying over the fate of one singular grain of sand on a vast beach. At best, the whole human race is as influential as the meteor that killed the dinosaurs – we might alter the climate and cause a mass extinction. But after a few million years – a cosmic blink of an eye – a bunch of new species will be roaming the earth, adjusted to whatever climate it has at that point. What difference does a singular human life make? We are born, we experience a few moments of joy mixed with a few moments of pain, we die. That's it. No big deal.

Some 135 years before the atoms making up Jim Carrey's body danced around Fashion Week in New York, the Russian author Leo Tolstoy realized he was nothing but a 'temporal, accidental conglomeration of particles' that would last for some time, before the 'accidentally cohering globule of something', also called his body, would stop producing the experience of life and instead start fermenting.[121] Around the same time, poet and philosopher Henry Thoreau wrote, 'I am a parcel of vain strivings tied; By a chance bond together.'[122] And some 2,200 years before Tolstoy, the author of the book of Ecclesiastes in the Bible reminded us that, 'All go to one place. All are from the dust, and to dust all return.' Ashes to ashes, dust to dust. Human life takes a pile of material, breathes an experiencing being into it and, after a few decades, the pile of material is returned to earth: 'Vanity of vanities! All is vanity. What does man gain by all the toil at which he toils under the sun? A generation goes, and a generation comes, but the earth remains forever.'

Vanity, the key word of the book of Ecclesiastes, comes from the Hebrew word *hevel*, which has also been translated as 'futility' or 'meaninglessness'. Literally, hevel refers to evanescent vapour, to wind, to man's transitory breath. It beautifully captures the transient nature of life: our brief life and our strivings are but a disappearing vapour in the wind.

Our existence is a brief blink of an eye between two non-existences; a momentary, thin light flickering from a candle. Just as you have started to understand what the light reveals, the candle is blown out. As Shakespeare put it: 'Out, out, brief candle! Life's but a walking shadow, a poor player that struts and frets his hour upon the stage and then is heard no more: it is a tale told by an idiot, full of sound and fury, signifying nothing.'[123]

Thomas Carlyle, the nineteenth-century British author and 'Sage of Chelsea', described this stage of realizing that nothing matters as 'the Centre of Indifference'. Carlyle's book *Sartor Resartus*, published 1834, became *the* book for a generation of youth seeking answers to life's big questions, inspiring everyone from Charles Dickens and Emily Dickinson to Herman Melville.[124] The popularity of the book stemmed from its role in 'addressing of the spiritual crisis of the time'.[125] At the heart of the book are three chapters: 'Everlasting No', 'The Centre of Indifference' and 'Everlasting Yea', which together provide one of the first full-blown descriptions of an existential crisis in the English language. The journey starts, as noted, with the Everlasting No, where all meaning is lost:

> To me, the Universe was all void of Life, of Purpose,
> of Violation, even of Hostility: it was one huge, dead,
> immeasurable Steam-engine rolling on, in its dead
> indifference, to grind me limb from limb.[126]

The fact that life is brief and nothing in it really matters can be a crushing thought. It certainly was so for Leo Tolstoy and Thomas Carlyle, who both went through a deep existential crisis where they temporarily lost their will to live. However, having pulled through the crisis, they were able to use this experience to build a new kind of spiritual conviction. The spot where nothing matters was a necessary middle station where one gets rid of old baggage, before finding a more liberating new world view. For Carlyle, Everlasting No led to the Centre of Indifference – which in turn led to Everlasting Yea, where a new way to think about the meaning of life emerged.

The fact that nothing really matters can be highly liberating. All your worries, all your crushed dreams, all your suffering, all the plans and projects that you must accomplish to feel good about yourself – none of it matters. You are free. Nothing binds you. There is nothing you have to do to make your life worthy.

The upshot of abandoning the old, outdated value systems is that there is no wrong way to spend a life. You dedicated your days to watching sitcoms and hanging out in the local bar? Good for you! You tried your whole life to become the local Pokémon champion but never topped the ranking? Too bad, but shit happens. You went all in on the 'who dies with most money wins' ideology, neglecting your loved ones, dying alone in a huge mansion? Not my cup of tea, but who am I to judge? You do you – and even though there might have been a plethora of ways to do you, good for you for having lived the version of your life that you lived. Nothing really matters, as Freddie Mercury sang in 'Bohemian Rhapsody'.

But why stop there? The moment where all old values have lost their grip on you is, in the words of Carlyle, the Centre of Indifference. It is the liminal space, the transition hall, between abandoning the old and growing the new.

Ultimately, there are two attitudes towards life that are needed to emerge from the Centre of Indifference. Regarding the past and everything that has already happened, we need the attitude of acceptance. There's no use crying over spilled milk. The Stoics called this *ataraxia*, the peace of mind that comes when we learn to accept life – and whatever it throws at us – as it is. Epictetus shaped this into a bring-it-on attitude: '"Do you want me to be poor?" Bring it on… "Do you want me to hold office?" Bring it on. "Do you want me to leave office?" Bring that on too. "Do you want me to endure pains?" Bring them on as well.'[127]

The grandiose-bordering-on-mental philosopher Friedrich Nietzsche went further and said that we not only have to accept whatever has happened, we have to love it. *Amor fati* was his recipe for how to live, which is Latin for 'Love your fate'. Your life is your life, with all its challenges, sorrows and peculiarities. So why not learn to love it?

All in all, you'd better accept the situation where your past life has brought you as it is. Because that is how it is. Your refusal to accept the past will not change the past. The moment you are in right now might be the result of some fortunate events, or some very unfortunate events. But, nonetheless, the moment you are in right now is the moment you are in right now. Accepting whatever has passed is wiser than struggling against something you can't alter.

So, whatever the situation, two facts remain true:

1. The past can't be altered.
2. Your actions might change the future.

So why not focus on changing the future for the better? On my keychain, I have a small metal plate with one word on it: *Meliora*. It is Latin for 'better', and American pragmatist philosophers such as Charles Peirce and John Dewey used meliorism to describe an attitude towards life where you are neither a naïve optimist nor a cynical pessimist. Instead, you are a meliorist who thinks 'the world is neither the worst nor the best possible, but… it is capable of improvement'.[128]

Many developments about the future are beyond your control. War, illness or accidents can strike anyone. The car that runs you over might already have started its engine. However, usually there is always something that you have some control over. Focus your energy on that – make an effort to improve whatever is in your hands to improve. Instead of focusing on what is generally wrong with the world, focus on the wrongs you actually have an influence over – through local action in your community, through voting, through taking care of your loved ones, or through what-ever means you have to change the world for the better. There's always something we can improve upon, big or small. So let's focus our thoughts and actions on the parts of the world we are able to improve.

When crisis hits, pessimism is paralyzing. Unfounded optimism is naïve and dangerous and can also lead you to passively wait for things to get better. The healthy option is meliorism: accept what has happened and improve what is still to happen. Learn not to worry about what you can't influence while focusing your energy on the smaller or bigger things that you can. Action is the remedy. Even when the world seemingly moves in all the wrong directions, there is always something you can have an impact on. It could be something small and immediate, like helping your family.

In a dire enough situation, the only thing you can influence is your own reaction to it – that tiny space between external stimulus and your response to it. Through concentrating on purposeful action, on doing what you can, you are better able to remain calm and sane while still capable of doing whatever is in your own hands to help yourself and those around you. That is all you need to – and indeed can – do.

Take Greta Thunberg, the famous Swedish climate activist. As a teenager struggling with depression, she stopped speaking and going to school, even refusing to eat at one point.[129] The lukewarm response to the acute climate crisis by the adult world made her lose sleep about the future. Then, with support from her parents, she transformed her anxiety into action by setting up school strikes outside Swedish parliament, which soon inspired a global 'Fridays for Future' campaign, leading her to give speeches to the European Parliament and at the United Nations Climate Action Summit in New York at the age of sixteen. Fighting for a better future has not only inspired tens of thousands of youths around the world to join her in this movement, but has also made the previously depressed teenager personally happy. As her father testifies: 'She dances around, she laughs a lot, we have a lot of fun – and she's in a very good place.'[130] No single person can alter the course of an overwhelming issue like climate change. But by doing what we can to be (a tiny) part of the solution, we remain active, energized and purposeful.

Accepting the past and improving the future: these two things we can do even after we have walked through the gates of the Centre of Indifference. Tasting indifference liberates us from the grip of past values. One option, of course, is to remain without values – to live in a cold, mechanistic world where nothing matters. The other option is to commit to some values. Not because they ought to be indulged, but because they feel worth valuing.

Passing through the Centre of Indifference allows you to be satisfied with your lot in life and oblivious to unhealthy cultural norms, which frees you to excitedly pursue whatever goals you have chosen for yourself.

Being human is being active. A life of leisure where we just lie around, passively waiting for the next meal to arrive, is not enough for us. We need some positive goals to energize our actions. As Viktor Frankl said: 'What man actually needs is not a tensionless state but rather the striving and struggling for a worthwhile goal.'[131] Beyond ensuring survival, humans are activated by 'the call of a potential meaning waiting to be fulfilled'. Realizing this starts the journey towards energized action.

This book is about that attitude, what I call **energized contentment,** where you are satisfied with your lot in life and oblivious to unhealthy cultural norms, while excitedly pursuing whatever project you have chosen for yourself. In the words of Finland's national poet Eino Leino: 'To dust you shall return, you can be certain / But you have time to burn till falls the curtain.'[132]

The rest of the book focuses on how to ignite your fire.

PART III: Start Living Your Own Life

CHAPTER 8

START CARING ABOUT
YOURSELF

On 15 October 1936 reporter George B. Garrott from the *New York Times* was waiting on Park Avenue, Manhattan, for the kitchen maid Sally Salminen to return to her cellar apartment. Along with other reporters, he wanted to know how this poor and uneducated maid from Finland had been able to write a novel that had just won the first prize in a big Nordic literature competition.

'Maid spent a year writing prize book' was the headline on the *New York Times*' front page the next day.[133] It was reported that Salminen, described as 'a quiet, charming young woman' with 'auburn, bobbed hair, a rounded face devoid of make-up, small nose and glowing, round, expressive blue eyes', had written the novel mainly at night, after her work shifts as a maid. She revealed that one of the most difficult things about this writing project 'was inserting the two dots over the a's and o's' to make an English typewriter write the 'ä's and 'ö's used in Finnish and Swedish.

Her award-winning and bestselling debut novel *Katrina*, eventually translated into over twenty languages, tells the story of a young peasant girl, the eponymous Katrina, who marries a poor loafer of a seaman and ends up living in a miserable hut in a small village on an island in the Finnish archipelago.[134] Katrina struggles in the village, where the men are mostly at sea and the captains own the land, and she labours at their mercy in order to feed her children, facing starvation every winter. The story drew inspiration from Salminen's own childhood growing up in a similar village of seafaring men on a small island, with her father drowning when she was seven, and her mother struggling to make ends meet with twelve children. One motivation to want to tell the story of Katrina was that 'so many novels had been written about the adventures of men that she felt there was something to be said for the women who stayed at home'.[135] Sally Salminen herself obviously hadn't stayed at home – she had, at that point, been living in New York for six years, working as a maid until her overnight rise to literary fame transformed her into a full-time author for the rest of her life.

A pivotal moment in her novel takes place when Katrina loses her only cow, her most valuable possession.[136] Hearing of her plight, a pious neighbour starts a collection and all the rich captains and farmers of the village pitch in. When Katrina hears of this, she gets irritated: 'They have no right to organize a collection without asking me first. I am poor but not a beggar.' Her neighbours don't understand her attitude. 'It's no fun accepting favours. But the poor have no other way… If nothing else, you have to be humble for the sake of your children.' Finally, the pious woman arrives at Katrina's hut with an envelope full of money and puts it on the table. They talk about other stuff first but 'the envelope burned like a glowing ember' in front of Katrina. Finally, when the woman offers the envelope, Katrina refuses to accept it, stating that she doesn't remember having asked for it. Alone at night she doubts her choice. Does she have a right to doom her children to starve the next winter? Is her dignity worth their suffering? But she decides to walk this path anyway.

When the richest captain and leader of the village, on whose mercy Katrina's livelihood depends, hears of her choice, he summons her to his office.

'Do you need a new cow?' he asks, visibly angry.

'Yes,' Katrina answers.

'Then why do you refuse the money for it?'

'I need a cow. But I did not *ask* for it.'

Now the captain is furious: 'You think you're too good to accept handouts?'

Katrina raises her head, locks her eyes on the captain and states proudly: 'Yes, exactly that.'

The need for self-determination runs deep in us humans. We want to be the captains of our own lives, rather than live at the mercy of other captains. We want to follow our own path, find our own North Star and steer our own course. Women have historically been denied this opportunity, forced by discriminatory laws to live as property of their fathers and husbands. Female authors through the ages have struggled to pave the way for freedom of self-expression. Mary Evans, writing in the mid-nineteenth century, had to adopt the masculine pen name George Eliot to be taken seriously as an author. In 1929, Virginia Woolf, who called George Eliot's *Middlemarch* 'one of the few English novels written for grown-up people',[137] wrote about the importance of 'a room of one's own' to allow women to have freedom of expression. Closer to our time, Susan David tells how her mother told her that it is crucial that 'you always need to have just enough money to say "Screw you"'[138] – just like Katrina decided to say 'screw you' to the alms from the rich captains, even if the price to pay was allowing her children to starve. For her, dignity and self-determination were more important values.

Sally Salminen wrote herself out of servitude and into freedom. Ulrika Gustafsson, an academic who has studied Salminen, stated that she 'could not become an author before she had stopped thinking like a maid, and started to think like a man'.[139] She might have been small and modest, but she had a fierce spirit, not afraid to speak truth to power, revealing the various ways women had been suppressed throughout the ages and willing to stand up for the values she believed in. She denounced the Nazi system on the pages of the *New York Times* in 1938, declaring that she was willing to 'combat it', became an outspoken advocate of women's rights and came to publish a number of well-received novels.

Having self-determination is the difference between merely surviving and truly living; the difference between slavery and freedom. 'Live free or die' has been a real-life choice for millions of people in various rebellions around the world who have decided to put their lives at risk to fight against oppression and for the liberty of their people. Throughout the ages, whether on a national or individual level, humans have attempted to escape various oppressors – from dictators, chiefs and warlords to bosses, coaches and spouses – in order to find freedom and self-determination.

Freedom as the Human Condition

'Man is condemned to be free.' This is how the famous French existentialist philosopher Jean-Paul Sartre summarized the human condition.[140] Here we are – thrown into a world where we can make choices and act. Not only *can* we make choices, but we also *must* make choices as we face various forks in the road, and have to decide which path to take – from trivial choices like what shirt to wear today, to life-changing choices like should I accept that job offer or should I message that person with the cute smile.

Cognitive scientist Keith Stanovich argues that this capability for reflective thinking is what sets us humans free. In his book *The Robot's Rebellion: Finding Meaning in the Age of Darwin*, he argues that simple lifeforms like bacteria or insects are trapped in executing the behavioural patterns programmed into them through genes.[141] Slowly, through evolution, some animals started to generate higher cognitive functions that allowed them to set goals for themselves. These cognitive functions are nowhere else as developed as in humans. And herein, in our capacity for reflection and making choices, lies the origin of our freedom. Choices, as

Ruth Chang puts it, 'are precious opportunities for us to celebrate what is special about the human condition… that we have the power to create reasons for ourselves to become the distinctive people that we are'.[142]

This quality of being capable of reflecting on one's life and making conscious choices leads to another key quality of human experience: we can have a relationship with ourselves. We humans don't just experience our lives, but we can look at them, as if from the outside, and have a certain attitude towards them. We remember our past and plan for the future. There is a 'me' whose past actions we judge and for whom we make plans.

This means that your relationship with yourself is your most important relationship. You are not just the 'I' for whom life happens, but also the 'me' whose life you can look at, evaluate and make plans for.

How is that relationship working for you? Have you invested in it? Are you behaving like a good friend towards yourself? It is time to focus on that!

Learn to Love Yourself Unconditionally

When you make a mistake, how do you talk to yourself? Does it start an angry monologue with biting remarks such as, 'You are no good', 'Why are you such a mess?', 'What's wrong with you?', 'Why can't you be more like your sister?' or 'You don't deserve to be loved'? Can you relate to any of these?

Alternatively, are you accepting and compassionate towards yourself? Is your self-talk more like, 'Don't worry, everyone makes mistakes', 'You did your best' or 'This is an opportunity to learn how to not make similar mistakes in the future'?

Now, thinking about these two ways of responding, what would you say if your best friend made a mistake? Which of the two types of responses would you react with? Would you blame or comfort? If you are a good friend, you would choose the latter approach.

It is unnerving that so many of us talk to ourselves in ways we would never speak to a loved one. Too many of us have attitudes towards ourselves that we would never have towards our friends. When did our relationship with ourselves end up on such a bad footing? That nagging voice in your head is *you*. And it is time for you to change that. How about becoming friends with yourself instead? How about practising some self-compassion?

Since 2003, psychologist Kristin Neff has spearheaded a research programme into self-compassion.[143] Drawing inspiration from Buddhist psychology, humanistic psychologist Carl Rogers' 'unconditional positive regard' and psychotherapist Albert Ellis's 'unconditional self-acceptance', Neff argues that self-compassion has three components:[144]

1. *Self-kindness* is about an attitude towards yourself where you are caring and understanding instead of harshly critical or judgemental. Instead of

relentless criticism towards yourself, it means accepting the fact that you are imperfect. When facing hard times, self-kindness means that you soothe and comfort yourself.

2. *Sense of common humanity* involves recognizing that, as humans, everyone fails, makes mistakes and feels inadequate in various ways. Rather than thinking 'there is something wrong with me', this attitude realizes that imperfection is part of the human condition – we all are imperfect, face hard times, struggle inside, do things we regret and suffer. It is all too human to fail.

3. *Mindfulness* is the third component of self-compassion. It involves the ability to be aware of the present moment without trying to edit out the bad parts. There might be things about yourself or the situation that you dislike. Instead of attempting to ignore, block or sidestep those aspects, you face the present moment in a balanced manner, also allowing room for the negative.

Remember *self-esteem*, who we hung out with in Chapter 2? Instead of focusing on whether self-esteem is high or low, we saw that it is better to think whether our self-esteem is needy or stable. Needy self-esteem is dependent on validation from others and, when others poke holes in our inflated self-esteem with criticism, we easily lash out to defend our all too vulnerable positive self-regard.

Another path to high self-esteem is through loving ourselves and accepting and finding ourselves worthy, no matter what. While self-esteem is a judgement of oneself, self-compassion 'is a way of relating to the ever-changing experience of who we are with kindness and acceptance'.[145] Through self-compassion, what we are building is more unconditional and stable self-esteem that is not dependent on others.

Self-compassion is good for you.[146] When you accept yourself unconditionally, you are less prone to developing depression and anxiety, and less prone to thinking about suicide. Instead, you are more likely to experience happiness and positive feelings. What's more, those with post-traumatic stress disorder (PTSD) have also seen an improvement in symptoms through being taught self-compassion. In another study, people felt less ashamed after having written about a shameful or embarrassing event in a self-compassionate way. Whatever adversities you are facing in life, self-compassion helps you feel less overwhelmed by it and more accepting towards the negative emotions it generates. You will still fail, but you'll feel less like a failure – you'll learn not to attribute it to your worth. This all makes you more resilient for whatever life throws at you.

Sometimes, people are wary of self-compassion as they think it will somehow make them weak and less motivated. In fact, the opposite is true. Self-compassion makes people more resilient when facing adversities in life and more prone to reacting in adaptive ways. Studies of soldiers have found that self-compassion reduced the possibility of PTSD after combat exposure, while also allowing the soldiers to function better in daily life.[147] Self-compassion is also positively associated with high performance standards and personal initiative, and predicts greater personal improvement after making mistakes.[148] As Kristin Neff sums it up: 'When going into battle, literally or figuratively, being one's own ally is going to make an individual stronger and more resilient than treating oneself like the enemy.'[149]

The good news is that self-compassion can be learned. Many studies have shown that consciously focusing on being more compassionate towards ourselves – writing ourselves self-compassionate letters, attempting to be more forgiving to ourselves and similar efforts – helps in making us more compassionate towards ourselves.[150] Therapy has also been shown to cultivate self-compassion. The bad news is, if your current way of relating to yourself is far from self-compassionate, cultivating self-compassion can take time and effort. If your brain has been in the habit of engaging in a blame-and-punish monologue any time you make a mistake, it will take some effort to root that out. Just labelling the monologue can help, as will recognizing it as that: a monologue of negative self-talk. Try to think of whose voice it has – perhaps your father's, your mother's or another caregiver's? The more aware you become of this monologue, the more you can build a healthy distance from it, and the less you will be gripped by it. When you once again catch yourself playing that monologue inside your head – and this will happen again and again – you can try to suggest to your mind that, instead of 'blaming and punishing', how about some 'forgiving and learning'? It is easier to learn from your mistakes when you look at them from a more neutral point of view.

In addition to unlearning the negative self-talk, you can also build self-compassion by cultivating a more compassionate attitude towards yourself. A good way to do this is to connect with your inner child – bring to mind that small, sensitive kid you once were, and approach them with sympathy and care. Then remind yourself that this child still lives inside you and show some love for the person this child has become – you.

As long as you don't accept yourself, you are not truly free. When your self-esteem is conditional on other people's approval, you remain stuck in doing whatever gives you that temporary boost in self-worth. By accepting yourself and being self-compassionate, you liberate yourself from such external validation. This makes it possible to be more sensitive to what you want to do with your life. Freedom starts from learning to love yourself.

Accordingly, the attitude I want you to cultivate is unconditional love for yourself. Self-compassion does not mean that you are deluding yourself. It means being deeply aware of who you are and accepting yourself as you are, including your most irritating and embarrassing traits and habits.

Optimally, learn to love both your past self and your future self. When it comes to your past self, have sympathy for it. Forgive and accept your past self – whatever mistakes or wrong choices they made. It is too late to change that now. If such choices still bother you, remember that the only thing you can change is the future: make plans about how to amend them by some future actions of yours. Instead of ruminating on the past, focus more of your energy on caring about your future self. Love the person you could become. Like a parent, nurture that person. Help to cultivate that better version of you into being. Think about what kind of person you could be. And then think what kind of encouragement could lead you to be that person.

Accept that change will not be instantaneous and that mistakes will be made. And still, commit yourself to cultivate that person into being. That way, you love your past self, your current self and your future self.

Do Whatever You Want

The best public sauna in Tallinn, Estonia, is Kalma Saun. Once there, enjoying the *löyly* – the Finnish word for the heat inside a sauna – I met the then chairman of the International Smoke Sauna Club, Seppo Leskinen. Now, Finns take saunas seriously. With 5.5 million people and 3 million saunas (almost as many as passenger cars in Finland), there is a sauna for every other citizen.

If you haven't been to Finland, you probably have never been to a sauna worthy of its name. The kind of windowless, heated rooms you find in international hotels are derogatorily called 'sweat boxes' in Finland. In the hierarchy of Finnish saunas, any electrically heated saunas are at the bottom. Real saunas are heated with real wood. And on the top of the hierarchy are smoke saunas that are heated with wood, but lack a chimney. During the heating, which typically takes around five hours, the sauna is filled to the brim with thick smoke. Only after the last logs have burned down and the smoke disappeared is it time to step into the 110°C warm löyly.

Enjoying the löyly with Seppo, I was treated to an endless stream of stories, facts and titbits about smoke saunas. After the chance meeting, I realized what a genius he is. Smoke saunas are his passion. And one of his main tasks at the International Smoke Sauna Club is to give certificates for smoke saunas. This means that he is constantly invited to various smoke saunas, not only in Finland, but also in Estonia and other countries. Seppo holds a diary of all the smoke saunas he has visited, and the number was 570 when we met. That is a record that will not be easily beaten – while I consider myself a sauna aficionado, my number is closer to ten. Nobody gets to enjoy as many different smoke saunas in the world as Seppo. And he clearly loves every moment of it.

What I love about the human species is the diversity of our interests. One person loves smoke saunas, another bouldering, while yet another is passionate about calligraphy. Different people love different things. Sometimes it is easy to trace where the interest has grown. A love for books, like the love of playing a musical instrument, is often passed down through generations – given my excitement for books, and me reading fantasy books to my children when they were small, it is not too surprising that my oldest son loves reading fantasy. On other occasions, a child develops a deep love for something that nobody in their family or even friends have been engaged in. Something just clicks when they first put their fingers on a fretboard of a guitar or learn that there are people who study insects for a living.

In that spirit, the general answer to the question, *What should I do with my life?* is simple: do whatever you want. Whatever floats your boat is what you should be doing. To hell with those who laugh at or ridicule your choices. Not supporting your choices is their loss, a testimony of their narrow-mindedness. There is no external constraint on what you should be doing with your life. You were not created for one mission written in the stars that you can't alter. There is no law commanding you to surrender to a certain path. If you are passionate about something, then do that! Life is too short to be wasted with meeting other people's expectations. You have a unique life. Live it in a unique way.

Having said that, there are a few caveats. First, exercise your freedom in ways that do not diminish the freedom of others. In other words, make sure your activities don't hurt other people. Second, there are obvious constraints on what you are capable of doing, depending on the country you live in, the money you and your family have available, the education you have received, your skills and abilities, and – in way too many places – your gender, sexuality and the colour of your skin will, unfortunately, also factor into this. A citizen of a Nordic country with a university degree and some money in the bank has completely different opportunities to exercise their freedom than someone coming from a poor family in a war-torn country like Afghanistan and Lebanon – which are found at the bottom of the World Happiness Report ranking. Sometimes merely surviving takes up all your energy. I am not saying that you should ignore the realities of life imposed upon you by your place in society. But be realistic about the ground you are standing on – assess your resources, the risks and the opportunities.

My point is that, besides the obvious constraints put in place by the fact that we need food, water and shelter to survive, don't put any *additional self-imposed constraints* on your aspirations. Do whatever you want – mindful of the situation you are in.

You don't *have* to do anything. Do what you need to survive. And channel any energy beyond that to the things you love doing. You do you.

Know thyself: What do you love doing?

Having accepted who you are, how about getting to know who you truly are, beyond external expectations and internal wishes? How about starting to live according to your own values and interests?

Of course, that is easy advice to give. But what if you don't know what those values and interests are? In my teaching, I often ask students to take a blank piece of paper and write down as many activities as possible that they enjoy doing. What I've noticed is the vast difference in the number of activities people write down. Some people are able to fill the paper in two minutes with as many as thirty activities.

Others write down two activities – and then spend the rest of the time sitting uncomfortably, trying to come up with something more. Sometimes this reflects a difference in how they were raised as kids. Some kids are constantly asked, 'What do *you* want to do?', 'What are *you* interested in?', 'How are *you* feeling about this?' They learn to detect their interests and come to realize that their own interests and feelings matter. Other kids are almost never asked such questions. Instead, their caregivers tell them what they should be doing, what kind of behaviour is expected of them, what activities are valuable and what activities are a waste of time. These kids learn that their own interests don't matter and might not be in touch with their values at all – they simply don't know what they want, as they have never learned to listen to their own needs and wishes.

Autonomy as a sense of volition and self-endorsement is a basic psychological need of us humans.[151] One crucial factor affecting whether we experience autonomy is the external world: do our parents, schools, bosses or societal institutions allow us room for our own interests? Do they listen to and respect us? Another key factor is our internal world: do we know what we want and value? Do we have the courage to put our values and dreams into action?

Regarding the latter, one trick is to just stop and think. Grab a blank piece of paper. Write down all the activities that you enjoy doing just for the sake of the activity itself. In my case, the list would include enjoyable free-time activities such as playing football, going to the sauna or playing with my kids, but also activities that I get to do at work, such as writing or discussing deep questions with my colleagues. Then, put a number next to each item: 1 means you don't get to do that activity at all, 2 means you get to do it somewhat but would love to do it more and 3 means you get to do the activity as much as you want in your current life. This exercise was invented by my close colleague and friend Lauri Järvilehto, and it is one path to more self-awareness about what rocks your boat.[152] Research has found that simply choosing one value that is important to you and writing a paragraph about why can increase both well-being and academic performance – especially among various minority groups who might especially need such affirmation of their own values.[153]

Another exercise to raise your self-awareness is to list all your current goals on paper. What are you striving to do in the next month? What concrete goals and aspirations do you have? Having listed those, go through each goal and think about whether it is a 'want to' or a 'have to' goal. *'Want to' goals* are the ones you are attracted to, the ones that you truly want to be doing – they add excitement, joy and meaning to your life. In my case, I love writing and reading, and want to occasionally listen to good music and dance along. *'Have to' goals*, in contrast, feel like something you must do, no matter your personal preferences.

Next, divide your 'have to' goals into two: *true 'have to' goals* are necessary for your long-term health and well-being – or the health and well-being of those around you. Think brushing your teeth or doing household chores. I have to shop for groceries each week to ensure that my family has food on the table, for example. These kinds of 'have to' goals are a boring but necessary part of life. *False 'have to' goals* feel like an obligation but don't actually contribute to your health and well-being. You might have been locked into these goals through some past commitments, through striving to meet the expectations of others or through following paths that you thought everybody ought to follow. But now that you realize these goals don't contribute to anything good – they don't help your survival or your thriving – how about giving up on them to free space for a couple of more exciting 'want to' goals?

The point of this exercise is to become more self-aware of your motivations. Do you have enough 'want to' goals in your life? Can you give up some of the false 'have to' goals to make room for them?

In the path towards more autonomous living, knowing yourself is the first step: become aware of your interests, values and dreams. The second step is to be brave enough to live according to these interests and values. Knowing the 'why' is not enough – you also have to 'walk your why'.

Live with Mastery

Five metres feels breathtakingly high when you look down at it from a diving platform. Having already jumped from three metres, my then seven-year-old son climbed to the higher platform and nervously looked down at the water far below him. After a few minutes of back and forth on the platform, he climbed down and we went and enjoyed the waterslides and other activities on offer. After half an hour, he wanted to return to the platform. Again, he went to the edge, nervously stared down, walked back a couple of steps and then went to the edge again. I climbed up to support him and, together, we tried to gather the strength to jump. But it was the stairs down again. Later, when we were leaving the waterpark, he wanted to go up once more. This time, he stared down for some ten seconds, took one step back, then one step forward – and jumped. Adrenaline rushing in his blood, he was glowing the whole way home, eager to tell everyone that he dared to jump from five metres.

As humans, we seek and thrive on setting challenges for ourselves. There is likely no human society where children don't compete against each other in sprinting, throwing a rock or spear as far as possible, or in seeing who can jump the longest and highest. If there is a tree or a hill nearby, kids will want to climb it. For me, if I go jogging or to the gym, I need to set a challenge for myself to feel motivated, be it running a marathon or lifting 100 kg from the bench. Yet it is team sports that I most enjoy doing. In my adult years, I've played football in the fifth and sixth divisions of the Finnish league. Training once per week, my fitness and skills are far from professional levels. However, the training and matches are still a great source of enjoyment for me. Dribbling past an opponent, giving a genius pass, shooting and scoring – I love the buzz that comes with all the tiny good things happening on the pitch. To be completely honest, I get lots of enjoyment and a sense of mastery from playing with my kids at home, too – even though dribbling past a six-year-old is not a feat to be bragged about.

No matter our skill level – whether it is the Olympics or playing with friends in the park – we humans want to challenge ourselves. We enjoy the feeling of mastering something, getting something done and being able to grow and learn – a sense of competence is a human need.[154] That's why we set ambitious, just-about-reachable goals for ourselves, and engage in various tough tasks for the sake of the challenge. Author James Michener put it well when he said: 'I like challenges. I don't mind defeat. I don't gloat over victories. I want to be in the ballgame.'[155] The same spirit is found in the official Olympic creed:

> The important thing in life is not the triumph, but the fight; the essential thing is not to have won, but to have fought well.[156]

Besides sports and other activities requiring physical endurance, a sense of mastery can be found in various forms of craftsmanship, be it drawing, painting, knitting, pottery, cooking or building a terrace. One way of losing the sense of enjoyment out of such hobbies is to take them too seriously. You start out enjoying the activity and are excited about how your abilities quickly develop, making possible increasingly impressive items, be it a sweater with a complicated pattern, an elegant cake or earrings made from recycled materials. You post a few pictures about what you did on Instagram and get compliments from people. This sucks you in, so you start a social media account for your creations, and soon the hobby becomes a chore, where you count how many likes your latest creation has gathered on social media. One colleague told me that when she went to a drawing class in London, it turned out she was the only one in the whole class who approached drawing as just a hobby. I am guilty of this attitude myself. Professor Richard Ryan has been an important mentor, collaborator and friend for me in the research world. He once told me that he enjoys painting very much. I immediately asked whether he displays his paintings in any exhibition or otherwise advances his painting 'career'. No, he replied; he intentionally does not want to do that, as he wants to keep it as his own thing – something he enjoys doing just for the sake of the sense of immersion and creation associated with the activity itself. Seeking success and admiration in the eyes of others can suck the enjoyment out of any hobby. If you paint, paint for yourself. What we need is not success but challenges and activities that offer us 'just manageable difficulties', as social psychologist Gilbert Brim puts it.[157]

Research on flow – the state of complete absorption in a task – has found that the optimal level of mastery requires a balance between the challenge level and skill level. When the challenge level is high but the skill level is low, we get frustrated. The task becomes overwhelming, leading to a crisis in confidence and a feeling of a lack of accomplishment. In contrast, when the challenge level is low but the skill level is high, we get bored. The task is underwhelming and routine, and our hearts are rarely in it. Optimal tasks don't underwhelm nor overwhelm, they 'whelm' just the right amount. They challenge you, require you to put in the effort, to fully concentrate, but still feel manageable. So find your own thing, practise that and enjoy the sense of mastery you get from the activity – no matter how good or bad you rank in the grand scheme of things.

Gilbert Brim describes how, after retiring, his father bought an old abandoned farm with several hundred acres of land in northwest Connecticut.[158] He set out to trim the bushes and thin the trees in order to look at his beautiful and tidy hills from the porch. After several years, Gilbert started to notice that the upper parts of the mountain were no longer manicured as they started to be outside of his ageing father's range. Finally, his father allowed the hills to be, focusing his energy instead on gardening, with plots of asparagus, rows of raspberries and many beautiful flowers. A few years after his ninetieth birthday, he had to give up the garden, and his attention turned to the little border flowers around the house and to large window boxes that required no knee-bending to cultivate. Even as his physical ability was decreasing, he always found some manageable tasks to challenge and keep himself busy.

Similarly, after retirement, my own grandfather put his seemingly endless energy into craftsmanship. His greatest accomplishment in this area was a wooden sailing boat he built for him and his wife to enjoy in the summers. Later, he built large, two-metre-high wooden windmills for his children to have in the garden. In his final years, at around the age of ninety, he focused his energy on building nine small, about ten-centimetre-high windmills for his nine grandchildren. 'From the mill-builder' it says on the bottom of mine. He was a man who constantly needed projects – from designing water turbines and steel mills during his work career to building wooden windmills in his last years.

In childhood, our range of capabilities tends to expand, and we require larger and larger challenges to keep our appetite satisfied. In our latter years, as these examples demonstrate, we have to go through the opposite process, slowly shrinking our challenges to keep them in balance with our abilities. However, the basic truth remains: at any age, at any skill level, we need just-manageable challenges – activities we can get absorbed in, that push ourselves to our limits and enable us to gain a sense of accomplishment. In some cases, these are grand challenges; in others, tiny steps. In all cases, they will be rewarding.

Live Your Own Life

Love yourself. Know yourself. That's how it all starts. Learn to accept who you are, accept that sometimes you will make mistakes, accept that you have certain strengths but also many weaknesses. Learn to live with yourself and learn to love yourself the way you are. Then learn to know yourself: what is it that rocks your boat? What are you passionate about? What are you interested in? What do you love doing? What kind of life advice would a good friend give you? What would you recommend that a person like you do in their life?

Having accepted and become friends with yourself, start focusing on the future: what aspirations make you most excited right now? Set goals in those areas that are just manageable for you. Then make plans to reach those goals. Then take the first step – today. Through this, you start living your kind of life.

CHAPTER 9

————

START CARING ABOUT OTHERS

Talkoot is an old Finnish word that translates to 'working together to do something that one would not be able to do alone'. When Finland was still a mainly agrarian society, a farmer or landowner might hold a talkoot for a big project at their farm, such as building a barn roof. Neighbours would gather voluntarily and put in a day's work to help, then celebrate with food and drinks. A month later, someone else might need help with spreading manure on the fields, and the neighbours would again gather for a talkoot. This tradition carries on to this day. Last summer, my neighbourhood spent an afternoon planting trees and tending to the shared green spaces. That evening, we set up tables and had a get-together to socialize and celebrate. While the food and drinks are the explicit reward for such talkoot, the most rewarding part is actually the ability to be together and get to know our neighbours by working on a project together. There was laughter in the air that evening, but it almost paled in comparison to the joy shared during the day's work.

A sense of community is deeply meaningful for us humans. We need caring social relationships and a sense of belonging. I don't think I have to go through the vast amount of psychological research showing the benefits of close social relationships for us because you'll most likely have already noticed that spending time with your loved ones brings joy and meaning to your life.[159] An overnight bike trip with my oldest son, going to a sauna and dipping into a lake with my spouse, swimming with my two younger sons, training with my football team and having a few beers with friends I've now known for more than half of my life – those are just a few examples of meaningful moments for me in the last few weeks. The unifying theme is that they all involve doing something with people I care about – and who care about me.

Human Being Is Interbeing

When we look at a leaf of a tree, do we see the same colour? Ultimately, there is no way of knowing. We have both learned to call 'green' the colour we see when looking at leaves. But I will never know how you actually experience 'greenness'. And you have no access to how my eyes depict it either. Each human experiences the world from their own point of view. There is an unbridgeable gulf between us. I have my background – the convictions I learned from my parents and from my culture, the childhood experiences only I went through – and you have yours. We will never look at the world in the same way. In fact, even words might have slightly different meanings to us, depending

158

on the context in which we learned them. You have your ideas about what 'happiness' means based on your life experiences, and I have my ideas based on mine. We use terms fluently in conversation, but do we actually know if we are talking about the same thing?

These thoughts about the ultimate separateness of human minds preoccupied me when I was an undergrad philosophy student. I will never be able to reach another human being, because we inescapably approach the world from different points of view. These points will never be completely merged, so a chasm always exists between our own and other people's minds. That was a thought that kept me awake at night in my mid-twenties.

Then, one day, I had a revelation. I can still remember the setting. It was some philosophy student party in the basement of an old nineteenth-century university building with brick walls and cheap beer. The thing I loved about these parties was that at one moment you were laughing and sharing the usual 'when I was drunk' student stories, and the next you were discussing solipsism, Immanuel Kant's categorical imperative and other serious philosophical topics. It was here, hanging out, that a few friends and I were once again discussing the grander questions in life.

I haven't had many 'eureka' moments in my life, but it was in the middle of a conversation at that party when the answer to the dilemma of human separateness came to me like a sudden revelation. We might never be completely united on an *intellectual* level, but we can be deeply connected on an *emotional* level.

'The insight made me sparkle. It led me to a moment of connection with these people close to me. Importantly, this connection took place in our way of being together, not in our speech – on an emotional level, not on a rational level.' This is how I wrote about the event a few days afterwards. The human way of being is interbeing.

Indeed, we might be separate islands, reaching out towards each other through language, trying to explain our point of view to others. That is likely a key motivation for doing philosophy, as a drunken 4 a.m. text from a philosophy student friend revealed a few years earlier: 'Philosophy is an attempt to reach out to other people.' However, we will never reach others through words alone. Explain as we might, a gulf of potential misinterpretation always remains. What I realized is that this is irrelevant. The existential loneliness I had suffered from would not be solved through rational thinking. Our connection with other people is ultimately a matter of emotion, not of reason. We form strong bonds with others. We *feel* as one, we *feel* there is a bond between us. We strongly sense that we are sharing a moment together – like during that conversation I was having at that party.

Virtually all theories of human needs have included a social need, whether it is called 'the love needs' by Abraham Maslow, who famously wrote about a hierarchy of needs, relatedness by Self-Determination Theory, which is currently the most researched theory of human needs, or the need to belong, the need for affiliation and the need for communion by a few other need theorists.[160] However, I feel that human sociality goes deeper than this. It is not just the case that I, as a separate, atomistic unit, need other people. Rather, who I am partially blends in with other people. I have a physically separate body, and I have my unique point of view, but when I think about *me* – about who I am, what I care about and what my world view is – this sense of *me*ness is already entangled with other people. I care about those I love in the same way I care about me.

As I mentioned in Chapter 2, I hung out with quite different groups of people in my twenties. I'd spend one day discussing David Hume and animal rights with philosophy students, and the next I'd be at a student party full of business students talking about start-ups and the stock market. And then I'd be at a hippie gathering ecstatically dancing to trance music, before travelling to St Petersburg, where I'd spend my time discussing politics with Russian students before heading to one of the city's famous underground clubs (this was in the early 2000s when Russia was still relatively liberal). Youth is a time of exploration, and my attempt to blend into different groups was partly intentional – I wanted to find out what kind of person I would be with these people. But this was not just surface-level acting. I not only behaved differently with these different groups, I was a different person with each of them. I told different types of jokes, took into consideration different issues and even valued different things. Nowadays, in my early forties, my personality is more integrated, but I view those youthful days of exploration as necessary for becoming who I am today.

When we interact with other people, it is not just two self-contained wholes who exchange words back and forth, like in a ping-pong match. Interaction changes who we are – both of our personalities are shaped by it. Certain parts of me come alive in the presence of certain people. I have a few friends who bring out a very extroverted, self-confident version of me, someone who likes to laugh loudly. Some other friends bring out a more contemplative, almost melancholic version. My life is richer, and my personality fuller, for having both kinds of friends. We are who we interact with. More tragically, when I lose a loved one, I not only lose them as a person to interact with, but I lose a part of myself, too.

Caring about other people is, therefore, not just a conscious choice to extend your sympathies to something external to you. We often do that as well – for example, when choosing to donate to a charity to help people you will never meet. But caring goes beyond that. Caring about people you care about is, ultimately, caring about the extended you, tending us as an interbeing.

Instead of Collectivism and Individualism, How About Relationalism?

Humans are herd animals. For most of our species' history, we existed in small herds and tribes. As tight-knit small units, such tribes tended to put the group before the individual. Similarly, in agricultural societies in medieval times, your fate was often sealed at birth: you were born to specific parents with a specific status within the group. Your lot in life and what you could become was largely determined by your parents' position. Your role was externally assigned to you, and you'd spend your life as a farmer, father, woman, citizen, and so forth. In each role, certain behaviours were expected from you. Slaves and peasants, with a few rare exceptions, did not become noblemen. And you didn't have much say in this. In a society of predetermined roles, you learned to put your outer role before your inner feelings. As a child, as a father or mother, as a family member and a member of the community, you had certain role-bound duties. And your task in life was to fulfil those duties – no matter what you yourself might have wished. Noble living was about fulfilling your role well. Failed living was not fulfilling the role you had been assigned. No excuses or exceptions.

Modern individualism started as a battle cry against the constraints of such a collectivistic culture where your position and possibilities in life were by and large determined by the time in which you were born. The static medieval society was increasingly replaced by a more dynamic and industrialized society in the nineteenth century. Democracy, mass education, entrepreneurship, urbanization and employment based on merit rather than who your father was – these new inventions made it more possible to actually advance and make choices in life. Simultaneously, philosophers and thinkers like Ralph Waldo Emerson in the US, Friedrich Nietzsche in Germany and Fyodor Dostoevsky in Russia were preaching a new kind of noble individualism where we should not take the values of society for granted, but rather craft our own values. Everyone should have the right to create their own way of living, to claim our own life into our own hands. In making choices about your own life, you should be able to listen to your heart instead of your parents.

Then something went wrong, and this noble individualism was watered down. Some claim that the horrors of World War I are to blame. Too many stubborn gentlemen followed their inner 'duty' to senseless deaths. Others see that Nazi propaganda stole the concept and transformed personal moral strength into mass obedience. As Roy Baumeister puts it: 'when it comes to bad PR, there's nothing quite like a personal endorsement from Adolf Hitler'.[161] Still others claim that the new consumer society and advertising industry with the slogan 'you are what you buy' transformed inner moral convictions into outer displays of identity.

In any case, what we seem to have now is quite far removed from the noble origins of individualism. The right to define yourself through finding your own values has been transformed into a right to define yourself through wearing certain brands. I have desires, and all my desires ought to be satisfied – that's what modern *consumer individualism* is about. We are 'a generation bred on a diet of excessive consumerism and bombarded by advertising', commented Professor John Pitts, leading us to a brand of individualism where we are not 'defined by what we did' but 'by what we buy'.[162]

Personally, I don't believe that a return to collectivism is the answer. I, for one, think that everyone should have the right to listen to their heart and follow their own interests and values, instead of having to submit to the interests of their parents, families or communities. However, at the same time, modern individualism seems to have lost the positive care towards others that was one of the more attractive traits of collectivism. Members of the family or tribe unquestionably helped each other because that's what you did, putting in time and money to help those most in need in the family or tribe. Talkoot is an expression of what is best in collectivism.

What we need is a synthesis of the best parts of collectivism and individualism. What we need is relationalism. It acknowledges that each of us is an individual with our own needs, interests and dreams. Accordingly, everyone should have the right to self-determination, to make choices about their own life. At the same time, it acknowledges that each of us is an interbeing, with our well-being and whole way of existing interconnected with others.

Relationalism could also be called *compassionate individualism*. Compared to consumer individualism, it puts less emphasis on what we look like and more on what we really feel like. We all have the capacity to be compassionate and care for others, but it is often hidden beneath the cultural propaganda that tells us that we should only care about our own happiness. Compassionate individualism is about being able to ignore these messages and instead listen to our own minds and hearts. And this listening will lead most of us to find more capacity for compassion than we were led to believe through just looking out for ourselves.

This explains the paradox revealed by research done in the US that found that 'people who were the most individualistic were also the most likely to value doing things to help others'.[163] People who were most individualistic were least influenced by the cultural propaganda and most able to abide by their own rules and values. As they followed their own path, they found the capacity to care about others – and this led them to live a life where they put more emphasis into helping others than those who were more obedient to society's structures.

Consumer individualism is reactive individualism. It is a feeble attempt to be individual by consuming the products that marketers say will make us so. Compassionate individualism is active individualism. In it the person truly listens to themselves to find the values they want to follow in life from within. The question is, which path do you want to follow?

Care about Others Wisely – Balance Is the Key

Selfish living is typically unwise living. When we harm our relations for short-term personal gain, we usually also harm ourselves in the long term. A six-year-old raging about 'it being a goal' when playing football with neighbourhood kids might get their way through sheer force of will as their peers grow wary of their constant arguing. What the child doesn't realize is that the invitations to play football might stop coming if they throw a tantrum every time they are involved. Others are such a key source of well-being, support and resources for us that ignoring them tends to backfire sooner or later.

Living too unselfishly is, typically, unwise living. Some people attend to other people's needs so carefully that they completely forget their own wishes and needs. Some do this in their relationships, always putting their partner's needs above their own, accommodating all their partner's wishes. Some do this at work, unable to say 'no' to any request, and ignoring their own core tasks in their eagerness to please others. Soon, some of their colleagues exploit them by dumping all sorts of tasks on their desk. Some pick up this behaviour in childhood, having learned from their parents that their own wishes don't matter, that they are here to serve goals set for them by their parents – or, alternatively, they model the behaviour of their self-sacrificing parent. Many have to unlearn this harmful pattern – women in particular are often taught to ignore their own needs from an early age. By learning to listen to your own needs, you can learn to stand up for yourself and be more assertive in carving the space to live according to your own values and standards.

As with everything in life, balance is the key here. Listen to your own needs – but also listen to the needs of those around you. Dare to care about your own dreams – but remember to also value the dreams of others. In giving to others, don't be a doormat who agrees to whatever others ask of you. There are people who will exploit you if you do that. Be with others, build connections and care about others, but do it on your own terms. Sometimes firmly saying 'no' is the best way to help a friend. Having someone's best interests in mind is not always the same as agreeing with them – if they are making a wrong choice, you support them best by warning them about it. Also, attending a concert by your favourite band that you have waited for years to come to the city can really be so important for you personally that you just have to say no to your friend's birthday dinner. We are interbeings – the more aware we are of our own and other people's needs, the better we serve ourselves and those around us. Sometimes there are no easy choices, but the more aware we are of each other's needs, the more we understand each other and the more we can find solutions that serve us all the best.

We have already established that there is no wrong way of living. Don't connect with others just because you have to. Instead, recognize that truly listening to your heart usually reveals that your heart also beats for others. The kind of living we tend to endorse and value involves other people. So don't make the mistake of giving in to your selfish tendencies, thinking that they will lead to the right path. Connect with others because you are already doing it anyway, and because it is good for you. Don't fall victim to the individualistic, isolated world view that paints an incomplete picture of human essence. Dare to be an interbeing and build connections with others. Tending to those connections is where the path to meaningful living is found for most of us.

Start caring about others. Not because you have to, but because you already do.

CHAPTER 10

———

START CARING ABOUT BUILDING A BETTER WORLD

Blinded by a bullet hitting his head, a young soldier needed someone to escort him to the hospital. The trouble was that his troops were surrounded by the Soviet army – so the task would require sneaking through the enemy lines hoping that nobody would notice them in the thick forest. Helge, a young lance corporal, was charged with the task, as the wounded soldier was his friend. With a map in one hand and the hand of his blinded friend in the other, he started the journey to guide them through the forest where enemy soldiers could be behind any tree.

My grandfather, Helge, was nineteen when the Soviet Union started its offensive against Finland in 1939. Guiding the blinded through enemy lines was only one of the tight encounters he had during the war. 'It goddamn hurt, when you saw your pal die next to you,' he once told me. While I spent my twenties partying and studying (in that order), he spent them in the trenches, battered by enemy artillery, defending his home country. Finland, with a population of 3.7 million at that point, should not have had a chance against the military superpower of the Soviet Union, with its 170 million people. Nevertheless, the bravery and sacrifice of the Finnish soldiers, along with their superior ability to fight in the arctic conditions, meant that, at the end of World War II, Finland remained an independent country.

What does spending your formative years in a war, with many first-hand encounters with death, do to the psyche of a young person? After the war, most men went silent, not wanting to discuss what they'd experienced with their wives or children. Some broke down, drinking themselves to death in the subsequent years. But for many – like Helge – the war instilled a strong sense of determination into their future lives. They were on a mission to rebuild the country, to make sure that the deaths and sacrifices were not in vain – that Finland would remain worth defending in the future, too.

When, at the age of forty, Helge was asked to become the CEO of a just-founded state-owned steel factory, the salary offered was approximately half of what he was making as a director of a private company. But he didn't hesitate to take on the new role for a second. For him, it was an honour to have the chance to serve his country. Money did not enter into that calculation. He was a man for whom work was a patriotic duty and diligence a central virtue – all because he felt strongly that he was contributing to the common good. His was a meaningful life as he had found something bigger than himself to serve.

While no one in their right mind would want to swap places with a youngster going to war, my grandfather had one thing going for him. At the dawn of his adulthood, he was given a clear mission: defend his home country. Those of us who have been born into more peaceful and affluent times don't have that privilege. We drift, we ruminate about too many options, we second-guess our choices and we try out different paths without being able to fully commit to anything. Sociologists even have a name for this: *emerging adulthood* – the period of life in your twenties when you are no longer an adolescent but not yet fully an adult.[164] It's a period characterized by a sense of being *in between*, switching from one job and one partner to another, moving around, being financially dependent on our parents, not really knowing what to do when we 'grow up'. Nowadays, people in their forties and fifties still regularly wonder what they should be when they grow up. So, it is not only you – it is a whole generation.

In the trenches, carving pine burls into wooden utensils as a pastime, while waiting for the next offence by the Soviet army where he or some of his friends would likely get killed, I wonder whether my grandfather suffered from FOMO – Fear of Missing Out – which so epitomizes our time.

What Should You Commit to in Life?

So, what to do with this unique life you have been thrown into without your consent? We have roughly 30,000 days to live – if we live up to the age of eighty-two – and the chances are that you've already lived quite a significant number of them. What should you do with the rest? What can you dedicate your energy to during the limited number of days you will spend on earth?

The basic message of this book has, generally speaking, been that there's no one thing you really *must* do. You are not Harry Potter, Luke or Rey Skywalker, Frodo Baggins, or Katniss Everdeen from *The Hunger Games*. The universe did not assign you a mission at birth that is slowly revealed to you – along with some magical powers. In principle, you are free to do whatever you want. If you want to dedicate your life to lining up torn newspapers in neat rows, go for it! That's the beauty of having been born a human – you have the freedom to determine what you want to do.

Yet, despite this freedom, I urge that you find some grand goals to commit to. With this, I don't mean a capital letter 'Purpose in Life'. That is mainly the stuff of fiction. What I mean is a bunch of more everyday 'purposes in life', plural. It could be as simple as stepping up to become the secretary of the local football club or doing some voluntary work in your neighbourhood. It could be about taking care of your grandchildren or babysitting your neighbour's kids to let the exhausted couple go out for dinner, just the two of them.

There's one simple rule for these purposes: instead of focusing on you, focus on something bigger than you. That could be your family, your neighbourhood, a local club, association or congregation, the city you live in, the nation you were born into – or some region far away or some group of people that others have forgotten. Or it could be about creating art, entertainment or comedy. Sometimes, your personal history will give you a cause – if you were bullied in school, supporting an anti-bullying programme could be your purpose. If your loved one suffered from a rare disease, making the lives of those suffering from the same disease better could be your purpose. Whoever and whatever you see as deserving to be served and helped, therein lies your purpose.

Why should you care? Why should you commit? Because to care is all too human. With the rare exception of some neurological disorders, we humans come with an inbuilt capacity to care about others.[165] When we see somebody suffering, it brings us down. When we see someone experiencing joy, it lifts us up. No man is an island – it is virtually impossible to be happy if those around you are suffering. On the flipside, being able to do something good for those you care about is one of the most sure-fire ways to experience a strong sense of meaningfulness.[166] Pursuing goals larger than yourself is also a good remedy against a narrow focus on your own ego, thus contributing to a more stable sense of self-worth.[167] You should think more about whether you benefit others than whether others praise you.

Sometimes in my university courses I ask the students to do three small acts of kindness during a single day. These good deeds have ranged from calling their grandparents and washing their roommate's dishes, to offering a glass of juice to the postman and guiding a lost tourist to the nearby church. When reflecting on the deeds afterwards, the students often note that it made them feel surprisingly good. And this is also what research – including my own –

has shown time and time again: being able to help or delight someone else makes us happier.[168] The path to personal happiness and a strong sense of meaning in life goes through finding something bigger than you worth fighting for.

Start Your Purpose from Where You Are

So where can you find your purposes? Thomas Carlyle had a simple recipe for a more meaningful existence: 'doubt of any sort cannot be removed except by action'.[169] Instead of a preordained God-given mandate, Carlyle believed that your purpose is found in the here and now, in whatever specific situation you find yourself in in the present. The best way to identify a bunch of purposes is to just look around you: work out what needs fixing, what could be better in the world around you, then figure out what you could do to address that. Therein is your purpose. As Carlyle puts it, just 'do the Duty which lies nearest thee'.[170]

You do not live in an ideal world. There is bound to be suffering, injustice, poverty and other ailments around you. In other words, things could be better if someone would just do something about them. **The first step** is to identify what could be better. What causes around you do you personally care about? What kind of joy would you want to see more of? **The second step** is to assess your own capabilities and resources: what are you good at? What special skills and knowledge do you have? What connections, social influence or monetary resources do you have at your disposal?

Then **connect the dots**: what is the most significant impact a person with your capabilities could have on whatever needs to be improved? If much has been given to you, then do much. Change the world. If little has been given to you in terms of resources, then do whatever little you are still able to do. Carlyle puts this in grander words: 'To each is given a certain inward Talent, a certain outward Environment of Fortune' and the task is to identify what is the best use of 'your combined inward and outward Capability'.[171] Ask yourself: **what does the world need that I could deliver?**

Identifying an answer to that simple question is where your purpose resides. The literature scholar Carlisle Moore summarizes this message well: 'Do the thing you are best fitted for with determination, and your practical and spiritual troubles will end.'[172]

Commit to the Process

Do you now have a purpose in mind? Good. Do you have several purposes in mind? Even better. Next, don't worry if you never accomplish them – that is not the point.

Success is fleeting; you can't ensure it. As we've explored in previous chapters, as long as you attach your happiness and worthiness in life to external success, you attach it to something you can't control. In poker, in business or any other area of life, what you *can* control is the process.

What this amounts to is an attitude where you need to commit to the process. When you've done the best you could, you can die in peace knowing that you've done your part. It might have led to a great impact, or, then again, it might not have. The important thing is you did your part, you showed up and you put in the effort.

'Don't aim at success,' says Viktor Frankl, because 'the more you aim at it and make it a target, the more you are going to miss it. For success, like happiness, cannot be pursued; it must ensue, and it only does so as the unintended side effect of one's dedication to a cause greater than oneself.'[173]

When my grandfather served in the Finnish army during World War II, Risto Ryti served as the reluctant president of the country.[174] When the war started in 1939, the then-president Kyösti Kallio felt that the country needed a cold-tempered prime minister. Ryti tried to refuse, but Kallio made him accept his duty. When Kallio himself then suddenly fell ill and died in December 1940, Ryti was inaugurated as the president, with the mission to lead the country through the war. In that position, he faced many tough life-or-death choices, where he needed to act quickly, with the fate of the whole nation depending on his decision. A wrong decision could have cost the lives of thousands of men and even the independence of the whole country.

A peace agreement was made in the summer of 1944. The conditions were harsh against Finland, with some territory lost, but, most importantly, the country remained independent. With an air of sarcasm, the Finns tend to say that the Soviet Union won the war, but Finland came second. After the war, the Soviet Union pressured Finland to take Ryti and other wartime leaders to court for leading Finland to war against the Soviet Union, and he was sentenced to prison. In his defence speech he stated:

> I have a good conscience. I have always aimed, to the best of my ability and understanding, to serve my country selflessly. I hope in some form to be able to continue to do so in the future. In the service of the homeland, it is not the place that counts, but the will. It may as well be in prison as in the President's castle.[175]

Your position is not up to you – as a president you have more resources and opportunities than as a prisoner. What is within your control is what you make of whatever is given to you. Purpose is measured in action, not in outcomes.

Purpose – Just Do It

Gioconda Belli was a young upper-class girl in Nicaragua in the 1970s, living the privileged life of a youngster from a wealthy family. The country was ruled by the dictator Anastasio Somoza Debayle and, as the oppression grew, Belli joined the Sandinistas, who struggled to overthrow the government. There, in the fight to liberate her people, she found a sense of purpose, mission and calling unimaginable to her in her bourgeois past:

Were we all mad? What mystery in human genes accounted for the fact that men and women could override their personal survival instincts when the fate of the tribe or the collective was at stake? What was it that enabled people to give their lives for an idea, for the freedom of others? Why was the heroic impulse so strong? What I found most bewildering and extraordinary was the real happiness and fulfillment that came along with commitment. Life acquired unequivocal meaning, purpose, and direction. It was a sensation of complete, utter complicity, a visceral, emotional bond with hundreds of anonymous faces, an intimacy of multitudes in which any feeling of loneliness or isolation simply evaporated. In the struggle for everyone's happiness, the first happiness one found was one's own.[176]

You might not have been pushed into a purpose as clearly as somebody having to fight for their life and those of their loved ones. But the world around you is not finished. By looking around, you will see many potential causes to commit to, many potential good deeds that you have the capacity to contribute to. Bigger or smaller, grander or more mundane, there's always something you can do. So go out and do it. Why? Because having some causes worth fighting for enriches your life by offering clear direction and energizing your actions.

One anthem I play to myself when I need some boosting up is 'Land of Confusion' by Genesis. The refrain of that song sums up the purpose-seeking attitude to life by noting that you are living in this world, no other, and you were given hands. Your task is to simply use your hands to try to make this a world 'worth living in'. We have been given hands – they are there for action. So go out and find something worth doing with them. Let's allow Carlyle to bring that point home: 'Up, up! Whatsoever thy hand findeth to do, do it with thy whole might.'[177]

CONCLUSION

———

THE DELICATE ART OF NOT CARING, WHILE CARING DEEPLY

It was a foggy evening in Oslo, Norway, on 28 February 1982, and the ski jumping world championship was about to commence. In that Nordic sport, you plunge down a take-off ramp at 100 kph, then jump from the nose of the ramp, soaring through the air for around a hundred metres, before attempting to keep your balance when your skis hit the ground on the landing hill. It requires exceptional recklessness on a good day and, this time, it was so foggy that you could not see the ground from the top of the ramp. You had to plunge into a white void, having only a few seconds to react when you finally saw the ground. Experts afterwards announced that the whole competition should have been postponed due to the dangerous conditions. Many of the top competitors failed, but the eighteen-year-old Finnish skier Matti Nykänen did not tremble. He jumped 108.5 m with the first jump, and remarked to the reporters that 'it's like jumping off the roof of a building with a sack on your head, you can't see anything', and then he was the only jumper to also break 100 m with his second jump, winning his first world championship.[178]

Matti Nykänen became a four-time Olympic gold medallist and five-time world champion in ski jumping, becoming one of the biggest sporting heroes in Finland in the 1980s. When I was five, I wanted to become a ski jumper, because that was the sport everyone was watching and talking about. His later life, however, was rather complicated. Alcohol played a role in various scandals – drunken mishaps and fights involving a knife – that the tabloid press was all too eager to report. At one point, he had to auction off his gold medals to pay off his debts. This tragic hero lived his life and his various love affairs (including five marriages) on the front pages of Finnish newspapers until passing away at the age of fifty-five in 2019.

He was certainly not a hero outside the ski jumping tower. He was certainly not a role model or someone you should take life advice from. He made every mistakes and committed several unforgiveable acts. But, at the same time, this uneducated man left behind sayings that the Finnish population has taken to heart, such as *jokainen tsäänssi on mahdollisuus* – 'every chance is an opportunity' – and *elämä on ihmisen parasta aikaa* – 'life is a human's best time'. Both of these are simple truisms, but, in their simplicity, they remind us that life, whatever form it takes, is indeed the best time we humans have – and the only time where we can seize the opportunities that come our way.

Behind the daring but shy boy who needed alcohol to socialize was some hidden wisdom, a certain attitude of tragic optimism, where someone dares to say yes to life in spite of everything. It's not what you have in life or how well life treats you. It's about embracing life in all of its colours, living life to the fullest and accepting that, whatever comes, this is the best life given to you. At least, it is the only life given to you, so you'd better learn to embrace it!

Life is the best thing that has happened to you – but also the worst. Being alive is a gift you received without any return or refund options. So, do whatever you want with this journey. No regrets. If you are able to live your life with a mindset of embracing what has been given to you, then you will have found contentment, no matter the external circumstances.

Cultivating the right way of approaching life involves accepting the present unconditionally. However, it also involves actively pursuing a better future for you and for us all through an attitude of energized contentment. How then to combine contentment with energized striving? For that, you need to learn about *kilvoittelu*.

From Competing to Playful Striving: Kilpailu and Kilvoittelu

The Finnish language makes a subtle distinction between *kilpailu* and *kilvoittelu*. While the first translates as 'competition', the second lacks a direct translation; it's akin to playful competing, like children playing 'capture the flag'.

The former is an attitude that many apply to their own life and the life of their children. Life is a competition, and your task is to get ahead of the field. Outsmart others in school, at work, in hobbies, in finding a partner. Don't settle. Always strive for more. Push, push, push.

For people stuck within competition, their life becomes a constant project. There are certain goals you have to reach. And all your activities are mere instruments to reach those goals. What you have unwittingly done is transform your whole life into an instrument, into a 'project ME'. As philosopher Thomas Nagel put it, we 'have an incurable tendency to take ourselves seriously'.[179] Our lives are shaped by plans, projects and aspirations. Too focused on executing the next steps of our plan to notice the beauty in life, we become mere empty vessels of instrumental striving.

In this project-based lifestyle, your life's value comes to be determined by how much progress you are able to make. No progress, no value. If you fail in your projects, this directly diminishes your self-esteem and sense of self-worth. In essence, you come to tie your own value to whatever goals you are striving to accomplish – in the worst-case scenario, these are goals you have not even chosen yourself.

However, while Nagel says 'we' have this incurable tendency to shape our lives into projects, we have to be careful in identifying who this 'we' is. In my view, this kind of attitude is especially strong among the educated, urban citizens of Western countries. There is this increasingly global monoculture of hard-striving professionals for whom life is a competition. No matter whether you travel to Chicago,

Vancouver, Paris, London, Singapore or Sydney, all you meet are similar striving professionals who watch the same HBO series and listen to the same music, who each can recommend the best ramen and sushi places in town to you. Despite surface differences in taste and career choice, each seems to have hammered their soul to fit a narrow project-oriented mould, to be able to join the clone-army of empty success soldiering. The big cities of the world have become one culture, where everyone seems to approach their life as a serious project, attempting to optimize their performance with whatever the latest productivity tricks are.

To break this bubble, we often have to escape the big metropolises of the world. When my travels have taken me to small villages in the highlands of Nicaragua, the non-government-controlled villages in Myanmar or the yurts of Mongolia, I have tended to find people who are happy with what they have. These people are not desperately striving to get somewhere – because they are already where they want to be. I remember a discussion I had years ago, sometime past midnight, with a man living in Runni, a small village in the middle of Finland. He was in his early twenties and most of his friends had left Runni for bigger towns and cities, as there were no opportunities for education and slim prospects for work in the village. He had also contemplated leaving but 'when the autumn comes, Runni is just so beautiful'.

Strikingly, while Finland and other Nordic countries have topped the global rankings of happiness, a recent study zoomed in on the village level, examining the life satisfaction of nineteen communities of indigenous people across the world.[180] Some of these groups, like farmers in the Western highlands of Guatemala or Tibetans in the Shangri-La county in China, had as high as or even higher average life satisfaction than the Finns, despite living in 'extreme poverty' by any economic metric. I put the extreme poverty in scare quotes here because, while their income levels justify that label, some of these groups live a life of abundance in having access to strong communities and high-quality locally sourced food, while living close to nature – something many Westerners with high incomes can only dream about. Even in Finland, outside of the capital, I've often been greeted by people who seem to welcome you with open arms and are not in a hurry, while in the cities, everyone seems to be desperately striving somewhere. It is refreshing to meet people who seem settled with what they have.

Competition or contentment? Often the choice is polarized into these two. Either you are constantly competing or you are so content that you don't strive for anything, passively remaining stuck where you are. Those defending competition as a lifestyle typically believe that, when you stop competing, you immediately regress into a passive do-nothing lifestyle.

The key here is this: competition and passivity are not the only options. There is also *kilvoittelu*, the art of playful competing. Kids play 'tag' or 'floor is lava' and, in that moment, they put all their energy into the game. When the game ends, however, they might forget about any wins or losses in a second. They were energized, they were excited – but they did not take the whole thing too seriously.

That's how you should approach life. Don't get passive; don't settle for what you have now. But don't compete either. Instead, kilvoittele; engage in playful competing where you enjoy the ride but don't take it too seriously. You will accomplish as much as the competing person, but with much less teeth-grinding.

Balancing contentment with playful striving for a better world. That is the sweet spot when it comes to different attitudes towards life. A wise student at our university, Eemil Rantala, just recently gave a speech about the pressure to optimize 'project ME' that young people nowadays face. He noted that, while it is a good idea to have goals and projects in your life, you should not take them too seriously but remember that much of life takes place beyond any masterplans. The ancient Stoic philosopher Epicurus aimed to express this balance by noting: 'do not spoil what you have by desiring what you have not: but remember that what you now have was once among things only hoped for'.[181] Derive happiness from what you have, while deriving excitement from what you could strive for.

Tapio Korjus is another Olympic hero from my childhood, having won the javelin gold medal in 1988. I was seven and, after lengthy negotiations with my parents, was eventually allowed to stay up to watch the competition, which took place way past midnight, as that year's games were held in Seoul, South Korea. I still remember his winning throw in the last round of the competition, the back end of the javelin flicking in the air, the commentator excitedly shouting: 'It is flying long, it is a gold medal throw!' Afterwards, as a coach to the next generation of athletes, Tapio Korjus said: 'An athlete should never be satisfied, but one can be happy all the time.'[182] Don't settle for what you have and strive for more. But, simultaneously, be happy about what you already have. Ville Juurikkala says that if you are in the water, fighting against the waves is not helpful, but you should also not allow the waves to passively carry you away. Instead, 'a surfer listens to the flow of life going along with the waves but at the same time strives through his own choices to steer his own course in life'.[183]

There is no podium at the end of life, which the fastest, richest or most successful climb. We all leave this life with our pockets empty. So, by all means, engage in projects. Take the projects seriously and put in the effort – but also laugh at yourself and your vain strivings on this tiny speck of a planet. In more mundane terms, *kilvoittelu* is about how to not give a fuck while also caring deeply. It is the art of combining two seemingly opposite attitudes towards life simultaneously: getting excited by opportunities, committing to projects, pursuing energetically whatever you have decided to strive for – but remembering that, wherever the projects are taking you, you have already arrived. 'Cuteness beats efficiency' is what my ten-year-old says when he is found petting the cat when he *should* be brushing his teeth – a bit frustrating when you're attempting to drop him off at school for 8.15 a.m., but hard to argue with, as his statement contains wisdom beyond his age. It reminds us that life happens in the here and now, not in the future, and it's in the here and now that you should be content with what you have, embracing whatever life has decided to offer you.

Put in the Work and Dare Greatly

This book will not change your life. But you can change your life with this book. Life philosophy is ultimately an art of practice, not mere theory. Teaching you how to approach life is like teaching you how to swim or to dance the tango. With words, I can explain to you the right moves, but the real learning starts when you jump into the pool or onto the dancefloor. It is by putting the insights of this book into action that you start changing your life.

In this book, I've offered you what I see as wise ways of approaching life. You may find some of the advice useful, some not. Be that as it may, the impact it will have on your life depends on whether you put it into use.

It's also worth bearing in mind that new ways of thinking will not stick the first time. Even if you consciously come to endorse a certain way of responding to difficult situations or emotions, you will find yourself reacting in other, less helpful ways. When that happens, don't worry. This is completely normal – nobody is perfect. Actually, you should be thankful that you noticed your misstep as that already shows you have taken the first step to becoming more aware of your own reactions. That, in itself, is progress. Accept your reaction and keep on practising. With enough repetition, the new way of reacting will grow into a habit.

Most importantly, dare to enter the arena of life and leave your own mark. Don't fear failure because the only way to avoid failing is by never trying. There is a famous passage from a speech delivered by US president Theodore Roosevelt in Paris, France, on 23 April 1910:

> It is not the critic who counts; not the man who points out how the strong man stumbles, or where the doer of deeds could have done them better. The credit belongs to the man who is actually in the arena, whose face is marred by dust and sweat and blood; who strives valiantly; who errs, who comes short again and again, because there is no effort without error and shortcoming; but who does actually strive to do the deeds; who knows great enthusiasms, the great devotions; who spends himself in a worthy cause; who at the best knows in the end the triumph of high achievement, and who at the worst, if he fails, at least fails while daring greatly, so that his place shall never be with those cold and timid souls who neither know victory nor defeat.[184]

That quote has inspired many. Nelson Mandela gave the passage to Francois Pienaar, the captain of South Africa's rugby team, before the 1995 Rugby World Cup Championship. Brené Brown's bestselling book *Daring Greatly* took its title from the speech. LeBron James, NBA's all-time leading scorer, has been seen writing 'man in the arena' on his shoes before many games. Tom Brady, NFL's most successful quarterback of all time, has taken inspiration from the quote since he saw it painted on a University of Michigan weight room wall in 1995, when starting college. For him, 'it's a constant reminder to ignore the noise, buckle my chinstrap, and battle through whatever comes my way'.[185]

Remember that there is an arena nobody else can step into other than you: your life. Nobody else but you can make the choices and put in the effort. Taking charge of your own life takes courage. It is often easier to just go with the flow, to default to the things that are expected of you. When you dare to follow your own lead, you expose yourself to failure. When you pursue something you care deeply about, failing hurts more. Maybe you don't achieve whatever you set out to achieve. Roosevelt's powerful words remind us that entering the arena of self-selected life involves dust, sweat and blood. It involves setbacks and difficulties. But then again, all ways of living involve these things. So, when you have found your direction, dare to follow it. You may succeed, you may fail. But even if you fail, you fail while *daring greatly*. That alone is enough to justify trying. The beloved Finnish poet Tommy Tabermann put it this way:

Those who come through the straight path, come empty-handed. Those who have trodden all the paths, come with eyes sparkling, scabs on knees, strange fruits in their frail sacks. So it is, my friend, so it is. Without getting lost, you'll never find your way.[186]

The Miracle of Life That Is You

The universe was cold and silent. Then came you.

Sometimes, when I wander through the streets of a city I rarely visit, say Santiago de Chile, I get into this nostalgic mood, where I look briefly at each individual walking past me, trying to imagine what their life is like. Each of them has a unique story. Each of them had a mother and a father, although some may not have known them. Each of them grew up in a particular neighbourhood, with particular siblings and friends growing up alongside them. Each of them has a unique set of people they love, with whom they have encountered things nobody else has. Each has both tragic and hilarious stories to tell about their lives. When they die, most of those stories are forever forgotten. So many stories, so many unique life trajectories even during a brief walk.[187] Then I remind myself of the millions of other people in the city or the country around it and experience a dizzying feeling. There are so many uniquely beautiful lives happening right now – each deserving a song, a book of their own.

It is a miracle that you exist. You have a unique point of view on life. Nobody else has encountered the things you have. Nobody else could tell the stories you tell. Nobody else carries the pains you do. But nobody else has experienced the heartfelt memories that make you smile. It is a miracle that the universe exists. What if there had been nothing instead of something? What if your grandfather had not gone to that gig where he met your grandmother? What if any of your great-great-grandparents had died before having offspring? The fact that you get to experience your unique life is a miracle in itself. Make the best of it. It is a unique opportunity; savour it. For the duration of your lifetime, a unique point of view is born into this world. And you get to experience it from a first-person point of view.

Here you are. You arrived at this moment through many paths, the years behind you having been rough or smooth. But, nevertheless, here you are. In this exact moment, still alive. This is the moment from which the rest of your life unfolds.

In the end, there is nothing you have to do. Nothing you have to be. Just be. There is no right way to live, no standards you have to surpass, no expectations you have to meet. Given our psychological make-up, such expectations sit deep, and liberating yourself from them can require considerable work. Try to untangle yourself from those deep-seated but ultimately unnecessary expectations. Learn to take life as it is. Enjoy life while it lasts. You don't get a second chance.

Jasu, a homeless man from Finland, captured what is essential in life: 'During my sober periods I've been contemplating and came to the conclusion that only two things are important in life: light and motion'.[188] Life is a pretty simple thing. There is a past, there is a future and there is now. The past can't be changed and the future is still in the making. The only moment where your life happens is in the present. So why not savour it, why not enjoy the tiny moments of meaningfulness it offers?

Accept the past. Improve the future. Enjoy the present.
That is all we need to know to live a good life. However,
to achieve this kind of serene yet energized way of living
typically requires abandoning several harmful life attitudes
that stand in the way. Some of them are biologically
programmed and some are culturally programmed into
our psyche. They tell you to focus on optimizing your own
happiness, to always do what others expect you to do, to
suppress or surrender to your emotions, to let your success
determine your life's worth, to worry about things you can't
control. Unlearning all of that requires becoming aware of
these attitudes that all too often unconsciously steer our
lives. It requires significant effort. I have aimed to offer you
some signposts that can help you find the right track. But
you have to put in the effort to actually follow them.

Don't take life too seriously. There is no wrong way to live
it, so just make the best out of whatever has been your path.
Learn to laugh at yourself. Learn to laugh at your mistakes
and your successes. From a cosmic point of view, both are
equally irrelevant.

Don't take life too lightly. This is your unique chance
to make your mark and experience whatever you want to
experience. Enjoy that, enjoy living. Love whatever shit hits
your fan. Wipe it off, and continue the journey. Your life
is not the best possible life. But it is not the worst possible
life either. It is your life. Make it yours.

ACKNOWLEDGEMENTS

Writing a book about good living is a lifetime effort. In writing it, I have not simply drawn from material read for the purposes of this book or from research conducted on the specific topics of this book – instead, this is a culmination of my whole life experience, drawing from insights I've gained both when I have had my philosopher's hat and researcher's gloves on, and when both of them have been long forgotten in the cloakroom, while I've been on the dancefloor of actual living.

Thus, the content and insights of this book have been shaped by all the people who have been close to me during various periods of my life, including my parents, siblings, friends, teachers and colleagues, and also various shorter encounters where a person met for one evening has offered something insightful that has altered or expanded my world view. In my previous book, I thanked many of the specific individuals who have played a major role in my life journey, and will now focus on acknowledging those individuals who have had a more specific role in the making of this book.

First, I want to thank my editor at Allen & Unwin, Erika Koljonen, for believing in this project and for her encouragement and many good comments during the project. Thanks also for Julia Kellaway for copy-editing the book in the last phase, helping to improve and tighten the delivery of my message. Similarly, I want to thank the editor of the Finnish edition of my book, Roosa Pohjalainen, for her flexibility, support and encouraging comments during the project. Finally, I want to thank my agent Elina Ahlbäck, for her and her team's support, dedication and good work in finding a publisher for this book in various languages, starting with English and Finnish.

I also want to thank the students of my Art of Living course at Aalto University, where much of the material of this book has been presented, and whose questions, comments and essays have provided many thoughtful challenges that have helped me to further develop my thinking around the key issues dealt with in this book. I want to also extend my gratitude to Esa Saarinen and Richard Ryan, who have both had a key role in shaping my thinking during my research career as one can see traces of their thinking in many places in this book. Furthermore, I want to thank the people who generously offered to read an early draft of the manuscript and provide comments: Miia Paakkanen, Harri-Pekka Pietikäinen, Lauri Järvilehto and Timo Tiuraniemi – thanks for many good points that helped in finalizing the book!

Finally, I want to thank my family: Piret, Vikkeri, Roki and Tormi – and the newest member, Minttu the kitten. Becoming a father has brought a completely new perspective on living and deepened the interbeing that is me, so thanks Piret for giving that gift to me, and thanks Vikkeri, Roki and Tormi for allowing me to be your father. Besides making me understand life from a new angle, you also remind me that beyond the academic study of life, there is the actual life to be lived and enjoyed in the moment. Thank you for being there, and for all the smaller and bigger everyday moments of meaning that you have brought into my life!

NOTES

Introduction: Are You Ready to Be Born for the Third Time?

1 Brown, B. (2010). *The Gifts of Imperfection*. Hazelden Publishing, pp. 5 and 35.

2 Existentialism is a movement that is hard to narrow down to any singular thesis. My take on existentialism is most extensively described here: Martela, F. (2023). Crisis of meaning in *Sartor Resartus* – Thomas Carlyle's pioneering work in articulating and addressing the existential confrontation. *The Pluralist*, *18*(2), pp. 80–106.

3 Sartre, J.-P. (2007). *Existentialism Is a Humanism*. Macomber, C. (trans.). Yale University Press, p. 29.

4 From the movie *Star Wars: Episode V – The Empire Strikes Back* (1980).

5 Drucker, P. F. (1963). Managing for business effectiveness. *Harvard Business Review*, *41*(3), pp. 53–60 (p. 54).

6 Having conducted research on human meaning and well-being for more than a decade, I have been surprised by how little we actually know. While there are certain factors that have been quite robustly shown to contribute to human well-being, much of the even widely circulating life advice has not been empirically studied. In particular, there are vast areas of human behaviour that have not been studied with rigorous enough randomized controlled trials (or quasi-experiments). So, while I will utilize scientific results to the degree that it is possible, and aim to ensure that my advice is aligned with the latest understanding of human psychology, there are many parts of the book where the relevant evidence is still missing, and we must trust the best-sounding advice.

7 This metaphor of three births comes from: Deresiewicz, W. (2014). *Excellent Sheep: The miseducation of the American elite and the way to a meaningful life*. Simon and Schuster, p. 86.

8 Kant, I. (1999). An answer to the question: What is enlightenment? In: Gregor, M. J. (trans.), *Practical Philosophy*. Cambridge University Press, pp. 11–22 (p. 17).

9 Kant's essay emphasized especially the *public* use of one's reason, thus operating much on the political sphere. Nevertheless, he also comes to lay the groundwork for freedom of spirit at the individual level as the goal of enlightenment, which was then further emphasized by German idealists and Romantics, and later on by existentialists.

10 Deresiewicz (2014), p. 85.

11 Ibid., p. 84.

12 Mark Lilla, quoted in Deresiewicz (2014), p. 85.

13 Deresiewicz (2014), p. 80.

Chapter 1: Stop Caring About Your Own Happiness

14 As estimated by the Global Wellness Institute: Global Wellness Institute (2024). Wellness economy statistics & facts. Retrieved from https://globalwellnessinstitute. org/press-room/statistics-and-facts.

15 Tsai, J. L., et al. (2007). Learning what feelings to desire: Socialization of ideal affect through children's storybooks. *Personality and Social Psychology Bulletin*, 33(1), pp. 17–30.

16 For the argument about happiness having become a cultural norm, see for example: Taylor, C. (1991). *The Ethics of Authenticity*. Harvard University Press.

17 Barbara Fredrickson's Broaden-and-Build Theory of positive emotions explains the existence of positive emotions by noting the evolutionary benefits they have for broadening our thinking and action repertoire and by triggering us to explore things, and thus building our capabilities and resources: Fredrickson, B. L. (2001). The role of positive emotions in positive psychology: The broaden-and-build theory of positive emotions. *American Psychologist*, 56(3), pp. 218–26; Fredrickson, B. L. (2013). Positive emotions broaden and build. In: Plant, E. A., and Devine, P. G. (eds.), *Advances in Experimental Social Psychology, Vol. 47*. Academic Press, pp. 1–53.

18 Moore, S., Diener, E., and Tan, K. (2018). Using multiple methods to more fully

NOTES

understand causal relations: Positive affect enhances social relationships. In: Diener, E., Oishi, S., and Tay, L. (eds.), *Handbook of Well-being*. Noba Scholar, pp. 1–17.

19 See, for example, Howell, R. T., Kern, M. L., and Lyubomirsky S. (2007). Health benefits: Meta-analytically determining the impact of well-being on objective health outcomes. *Health Psychology Review*, *1*(1), pp. 83–136; for various benefits of positive emotions, see, for example, the following reviews: Lyubomirsky, S., King, L., and Diener, E. (2005). The benefits of frequent positive affect: Does happiness lead to success? *Psychological Bulletin*, *131*(6), pp. 803–55; Diener, E., Lucas, R. E., and Oishi, S. (2018). Advances and open questions in the science of subjective well-being. *Collabra: Psychology*, *4*(1), pp. 1–49.

20 The quote is from the following blog post where Grant goes through the evidence for why trying to be happy could make us unhappy: Grant, A. (14 May 2013). Does trying to be happy makes us unhappy? [blog]. Psychology Today. Retrieved from https://www. psychologytoday.com/intl/ blog/give-and-take/201305/ does-trying-be-happy-make-us-unhappy.

21 The reference to the study is found in the next note. This quote is from the press release of the study: Chee, B. (1 May 2013). Today's teens: More materialistic, less willing to work. San Diego State University. Retrieved from https://www.sdsu.edu/ news/2013/05/todays-teens- more-materialistic-less-willing- work.

22 Twenge, J. M., and Kasser, T. (2013). Generational changes in materialism and work centrality, 1976–2007: Associations with temporal changes in societal insecurity and materialistic role modeling. *Personality and Social Psychology Bulletin*, *39*(7), pp. 883–97.

23 For one of the original studies, see Kasser, T., and Ryan, R. M. (1996). Further examining the American dream: Differential correlates of intrinsic and extrinsic goals. *Personality and Social Psychology Bulletin*, *22*(3), pp. 280–7; for a recent meta-analysis of the studies on the topic, see Bradshaw, E. L., et al. (2023). A meta-analysis of the dark side of the American dream: Evidence for the universal wellness costs of prioritizing extrinsic over intrinsic goals. *Journal of Personality and Social Psychology*, *124*(4), pp. 873–99.

201

24 This study is from the following
paper: Mauss, I. B., et al.
(2011). Can seeking happiness
make people unhappy?
Paradoxical effects of valuing
happiness. *Emotion*, *11*(4),
pp. 807–15.

25 The original study is
Mauss, I. B., et al. (2011);
several studies have since come
to the same conclusion, see
the following recent review:
Zerwas, F. K., and Ford, B.
Q. (2021). The paradox of
pursuing happiness. *Current
Opinion in Behavioral Sciences*,
39, pp. 106–12.

26 Weiner, E. (2008). *The
Geography of Bliss*. Hachette
Book Group, p. 318.

27 Ringer, R. (2013). *Looking Out
for #1: How to get from where
you are now to where you want to
be in life*. Skyhorse Publishing.

28 'Provided your actions do not
violate the rights of others', he
adds as a moral constraint to the
pursuit of greatest amount of
happiness over the long term for
yourself. Ringer (2013), p. ix.

29 Mauss, I. B., et al. (2012).
The pursuit of happiness can
be lonely. *Emotion*, *12*(5), ·
pp. 908–12.

30 Tan, H. B., and Forgas, J. P.
(2010). When happiness makes
us selfish, but sadness makes
us fair: Affective influences
on interpersonal strategies in
the dictator game. *Journal of
Experimental Social Psychology*,
46(3), pp. 571–6.

31 Putnam, R. D. (2001). *Bowling
Alone: The collapse and revival
of American community*. Simon
and Schuster.

32 Tennyson, A. (1994). *The
Collected Poems of Alfred Lord
Tennyson*. Wordsworth, p. 300.

33 Dejonckheere, E., et al. (2022).
Perceiving societal pressure
to be happy is linked to poor
well-being, especially in happy
nations. *Scientific Reports*,
12(1514).

34 Dejonckheere, E., and
Bastian, B. (2021). Perceiving
social pressure not to feel
negative is linked to a more
negative self-concept. *Journal
of Happiness Studies*, *22*(2),
pp. 667–79; Bastian, B., et
al. (2012). Feeling bad about
being sad: The role of social
expectancies in amplifying
negative mood. *Emotion*, *12*(1),
pp. 69–80; Dejonckheere, E.,
et al. (2017). Perceiving social
pressure not to feel negative
predicts depressive symptoms
in daily life. *Depression and
Anxiety*, *34*(9), pp. 836–44;
McGuirk, L., et al. (2018).
Does a culture of happiness
increase rumination over failure?
Emotion, *18*(5), pp. 755–64.

35 I wrote about this in *Scientific
American Mind* at that time:
Martela, F. (2018). Finland
is the happiest country in the

world, and Finns aren't happy about it. *Scientific American Mind*, *29*, pp. 44–6.

36 See: Marian, J. (n.d.). Number of metal bands per capita in Europe. Retrieved from https://jakubmarian.com/number-of-metal-bands-per-capita-in-europe.

37 On the general role of emotions in human life, see: Baumeister, R. F., et al. (2001). Bad is stronger than good. *Review of General Psychology*, *5*(4), pp. 323–70.

38 Martin, L. R., et al. (2002). A life course perspective on childhood cheerfulness and its relation to mortality risk. *Personality and Social Psychology Bulletin*, *28*(9), pp. 1155–65.

39 Kay, J. (2010). *Obliquity: Why our goals are best achieved indirectly*. Profile Books.

40 David, S. (2016). *Emotional Agility*. Penguin Life, p. 55.

41 Mill, J. S. (1874). *Autobiography*. Longmans, Green, Reader, and Dyer, p. 142.

Chapter 2: Stop Caring About What Others Think

42 By the way, how did I decide to talk about karaoke bars here? Because just yesterday I spent the evening in one. Along with a number of Finnish evergreens, I took a chance on Pulp's 'Disco 2000' and Macklemore & Ryan

Lewis's 'Can't Hold Us' (my peculiarity is that I like to do rapping in karaoke bars).

43 This distinction is from organismic integration theory, a sub-theory within self-determination theory. What I call external and internal control are called 'external regulation' and 'introjected regulation' in the theory, but here I wanted to use less technical names for them.

44 Deci, E. L., and Ryan, R. M. (2000). The 'what' and 'why' of goal pursuits: Human needs and the self-determination of behavior. *Psychological Inquiry*, *11*(4), pp. 227–68; Ryan, R. M., and Deci, E. L. (2017). *Self-Determination Theory: Basic psychological needs in motivation, development, and wellness*. Guilford Press.

45 For theory and evidence of human self-domestication, see, for example, Leach, H. M. (2003). Human domestication reconsidered. *Current Anthropology*, *44*(3), pp. 349–68; Theofanopoulou, C., et al. (2017). Self-domestication in Homo sapiens: Insights from comparative genomics. *PLOS ONE*, *12*(10).

46 These different types of motivation are examined in the organismic integration theory, a sub-theory within self-determination theory. The

theory proposes a motivation continuum with a number of different types of motivation ranging from amotivation and controlled motivations to more autonomous forms of motivation. Ryan and Deci (2017); Deci and Ryan (2000).

47 See, Henrich, J., Heine, S. J., and Norenzayan, A. (2010). The weirdest people in the world? *Behavioral and Brain Sciences*, *33*(2–3), pp. 61–83; Apicella, C., Norenzayan, A., and Henrich, J. (2020). Beyond WEIRD: A review of the last decade and a look ahead to the global laboratory of the future. *Evolution and Human Behavior*, *41*(5), pp. 319–29.

48 Leary, M. R., and Baumeister, R. F. (2000). The nature and function of self-esteem: Sociometer theory. *Advances in Experimental Social Psychology*, *32*, pp. 1–62 (p. 9).

49 Baumeister, R. F., et al. (2003). Does high self-esteem cause better performance, interpersonal success, happiness, or healthier lifestyles? *Psychological Science in the Public Interest*, *4*(1), pp. 1–44.

50 Crocker, J., and Nuer, N. (2003). The insatiable quest for self-worth. *Psychological Inquiry*, *14*(1), pp. 31–34 (p. 31).

51 Ryan, R. M., and Brown, K. W. (2003). Why we don't need self-esteem: On fundamental needs, contingent love, and mindfulness. *Psychological Inquiry*, *14*(1), pp. 71–6; Deci, E. L., and Ryan, R. M. (1995). Human autonomy: The basis for true self-esteem. In: Kernis, M. H. (ed.), *Efficacy, Agency, and Self-esteem*. Plenum, pp. 31–49; Kernis, M. H. (2003). Toward a conceptualization of optimal self-esteem. *Psychological Inquiry*, *14*(1), pp. 1–26; see also Crocker, J., and Knight, K. M. (2005). Contingencies of self-worth. *Current Directions in Psychological Science*, *14*(4), pp. 200–203.

52 Ryan and Brown (2003), p. 72.

53 Niiya, Y., Crocker, J., and Bartmess, E. N. (2004). From vulnerability to resilience: Learning orientations buffer contingent self-esteem from failure. *Psychological Science*, *15*(12), pp. 801–805; see also, Crocker and Knight (2005).

54 Leino, E. (1900). *Hiihtäjän Virsiä*. Otava, p. 84.

55 Ejrnæs, A., and Greve, B. (2017). Your position in society matters for how happy you are. *International Journal of Social Welfare*, *26*(3), pp. 206–17.

56 Ejrnæs and Greve (2017); Delhey, J., et al. (2022). Who values status seeking? A cross-European comparison of social gradients and societal

conditions. *European Societies*, *24*(1), pp. 29–60.

57 Delhey, J., and Dragolov, G. (2014). Why inequality makes Europeans less happy: The role of distrust, status anxiety, and perceived conflict. *European Sociological Review*, *30*(2), pp. 151–65.

58 Kishimi, I., and Koga, F. (2019). *The Courage to Be Disliked: The Japanese phenomenon that shows you how to change your life and achieve real happiness*. Allen & Unwin, p. 156.

59 Ibid., p. 116.

Chapter 3: Stop Caring About How You Feel

60 It is debatable whether anger 'pumps adrenaline into our body' or whether adrenaline pumped into our body (combined with certain other factors) gives rise to the experience of anger. The sequence of events is complex and interdependent. Nevertheless, situations that elicit anger give rise to both the bodily response and the emotions. See, for example, Haller, J., Makara, G. B., and Kruk, M. R. (1997). Catecholaminergic involvement in the control of aggression: Hormones, the peripheral sympathetic, and central noradrenergic systems.

Neuroscience & Biobehavioral Reviews, *22*(1), pp. 85–97.

61 For the effect of positive emotions in making us more open, see Fredrickson (2013).

62 The exact number of basic emotions is an open question, but happiness, sadness, fear, anger and disgust are most often included in various models. Love, interest and surprise are somewhat more debated. See Tracy, J. L., and Randles, D. (2011). Four models of basic emotions: A review of Ekman and Cordaro, Izard, Levenson, and Panksepp and Watt. *Emotion Review*, *3*(4), pp. 397–405; Elfenbein, H. A., and Ambady, N. (2002). On the universality and cultural specificity of emotion recognition: A meta-analysis. *Psychological Bulletin*, *128*(2), pp. 203–35; Ekman, P. (1992). An argument for basic emotions. *Cognition and Emotion*, *6*(3–4), pp. 169–200.

63 David (2016), pp. 2–3.

64 Frijda, N. H. (1988). The laws of emotion. *American Psychologist*, *43*(5), pp. 349–58 (p. 349, emphasis added).

65 See, for example, Welzl, H., D'Adamo, P., and Lipp, H.-P. (2001). Conditioned taste aversion as a learning and memory paradigm. *Behavioural Brain Research*, *125*(1), pp. 205–13.

66 Note that compared to Ward's translation, I took the liberty of changing 'maman' to 'mother' as the former is a strange word, and I also switched the word order of the second sentence. Camus, A. (1989). *The Stranger*. Ward, M. (trans.). Vintage International, p. 3.

67 David (2016), p. 4.

68 Tamir, M., and Ford, B. Q. (2012). Should people pursue feelings that feel good or feelings that do good? Emotional preferences and well-being. *Emotion*, *12*(5), p. 1061.

69 For benefits of negative emotions, see Forgas, J. P. (2013). Don't worry, be sad! On the cognitive, motivational, and interpersonal benefits of negative mood. *Current Directions in Psychological Science*, *22*(3), pp. 225–32.

70 David (2016), p. 170.

71 Ibid., p. 42.

72 For a discussion of various fight and flight strategies against emotions, see Harris, R. (2022). *The Happiness Trap: How to stop struggling and start living*. Robinson, pp. x, 44–5 and 246.

73 See Robert Webb's interview: Channel 4 News (30 Aug. 2017). Peep Show star Robert Webb: don't say 'man up' [video]. YouTube. Retrieved from https://www.youtube.com/watch?v=4A4KHm3brJE.

74 Harris (2022), p. 65.

75 Harris, R., and Aisbett, B. (2016). *The Happiness Trap Pocketbook*. Robinson, p. 99.

76 This builds on the saying 'It is not about feeling better – it is about getting better at feeling.' It is hard to track who said it originally, one potential origin is this post by Michael Brown: Brown, M. (n.d.). Am I going to give up… again? The Presence Process Portal. Retrieved from https://www.thepresenceprocessportal.com/resources/Giving%20Up%20Again.htm.

77 Covey, S. (1995). *First Things First*. Fireside, p. 59. Note that Covey presents this as the essence of an idea that he encountered in a book he chanced to open in a library. In some other places he has attributed a similar idea to Viktor Frankl but no such quote has been found in Frankl's books.

Chapter 4: Stop Caring About Your Past

78 This topic is talked about by Kishimi and Koga (2019), p. 67.

79 For women's situation in Afghanistan, see, for example, Kelly, A. (9 Oct. 2024). What is gender apartheid – and can anything be done to stop it? *Guardian*. Retrieved from https://www.theguardian.com/

global-development/2024/oct/09/what-is-gender-apartheid-activists-international-law-women-girls-rights-afghanistan-iran.

80 Frankl, V. E. (1985). *Man's Search for Meaning: An introduction to logotherapy*. Lasch, I. (trans.). Washington Square Press, p. 86.

81 Ansbacher, H. L., and Ansbacher, R. R. (eds.) (1964). *The Individual Psychology of Alfred Adler: A systematic presentation in selections from his writings*. Harper & Row, p. 176.

82 Epictetus. Encheiridion. In: Long, A. A. (ed.). *How to be Free: An ancient guide to the Stoic life*. Princeton University Press, p. 27.

83 LaFollette, H. (2001). Pragmatic Ethics. In: LaFollette, H. (ed.). *The Blackwell Guide to Ethical Theory*. Blackwell Publishers, p. 409.

84 LaFollette, (2001), p. 409. Note that 'blacks' in the original quote has been changed to 'Black people' as terminology has evolved since that text was written more than twenty years ago.

85 Mark, K. M., et al. (2018). Post-traumatic growth in the military: A systematic review. *Occupational and Environmental Medicine*, 75(12), pp. 904–15.

86 For factors promoting post-traumatic growth, see

Henson, C., Truchot, D., and Canevello, A. (2021). What promotes post traumatic growth? A systematic review. *European Journal of Trauma & Dissociation*, 5(4).

87 Solzhenitsyn, A. I. (1973). *The Gulag Archipelago: Volume I*. Whitney, T. P. (trans.). Harper & Row, p. 168; the second quote is from Solzhenitsyn, A. I. (1973). *The Gulag Archipelago: Volume II*. Whitney, T. P. (trans.). Harper & Row, p. 615.

88 See, for example, this *Foreign Policy* article: Michel, C. (7 Apr. 2024). How Aleksandr Solzhenitsyn became Putin's spiritual guru. *Foreign Policy*. Retrieved from https://foreignpolicy.com/2024/04/07/putin-russia-nationalism-solzhenitsyn-became-putins-spiritual-guru-ukraine.

89 Dewey, J. (1998). *The Essential Dewey, Volume 2: Ethics, logic, psychology*. Indiana University Press, p. 353.

90 Solzhenitsyn (1973) (Volume II), p. 615.

Chapter 5: Stop Caring About What Happens in the World

91 Aurelius, M. (2003). *Meditations*. Hays, G. (trans.). Modern Library, p. 48.

92 This quote, unlike the other Aurelius quotes, is from this book: McLynn, Frank (2009): Marcus Aurelius: Warrior,

philosopher, emperor. The Bodley Head, London, p. xiii

93 Aurelius (2003), p. 152.

94 Aurelius (2003), p. 152.

95 Singer, M. A. (2022). *Living Untethered: Beyond the human predicament* (1st edition). New Harbinger Publications.

96 Aurelius (2003), p. 45.

97 Quoted in *The Atlantic*: Lavine, R. (11 Aug. 2012). Iceland: Superlative happiness on a cold little rock. *The Atlantic*. Retrieved from https://www.theatlantic.com/health/archive/2012/08/iceland-superlative-happiness-on-a-cold-little-rock/261005.

98 A speech given by Jyri Häkämies: Häkämies, J. (6 Sep. 2007). Minister of Defence Jyri Häkämies at CSIS in Washington. Puolustusministeriö. Retrieved from https://www.defmin.fi/en/topical/speeches/minister_of_defence_jyri_hakamies_at_csis_in_washington.3335.news. Translation by the author.

99 From a famous speech J. K. Paasikivi gave 6 December 1944, on the occasion of the Finnish Independence Day. Translation by the author.

100 From the same speech as above.

101 Aurelius (2003), p. 48.

102 Aurelius (2003), p. 157. Aurelius attributes this technique to Epictetus.

103 Aurelius (2003), p. 148.

104 For an introduction to Acceptance and Commitment Therapy, see these two books: Hayes, S. C. (2020). *A Liberated Mind: How to pivot toward what matters*. Penguin and Harris, R. (2019). *ACT Made Simple: An easy-to-read primer on acceptance and commitment therapy*. New Harbinger Publications; for a more scientific summary, here's one article: Hayes, S. C., et al. (2006). Acceptance and commitment therapy: Model, processes and outcomes. *Behaviour Research and Therapy*, *44*(1), pp. 1–25.

Chapter 6: Stop Caring About Your Future Success

105 Ville Juurikkala tells his story in his book: Juurikkala, V. (2024). *Irti – Hollywoodista Santiagon tielle*. Like. Translations by the author.

106 Juurikkala 2024, p. 59.

107 Juurikkala 2024, p. 198.

108 Iikka Kokko's story is told in *Helsingin Sanomat* (1 Jun. 2024). Unfortunately, it is only available in Finnish: https://www.hs.fi/suomi/art-2000010459247.html. Translation by the author.

109 Quote from the above article.

110 Martela, F. (18 Dec. 2023). The outsized benefits of 'minimalist' leadership. *Harvard*

Business Review. Retrieved from https://hbr.org/2023/12/the-outsized-benefits-of-minimalist-leadership.

111 See: https://frankmartela.fi/2011/12/13/how-is-your-bucket-list-doing-want-to-know-what-are-the-20-items-i-want-to-do-before-i-die/.

112 The image and the 'Excited, not nervous' quote are to be found in this article: Saner, E. (10 Jul. 2018). How the psychology of the England football team could change your life. *Guardian*. Retrieved from https://www.theguardian.com/football/2018/jul/10/psychology-england-football-team-change-your-life-pippa-grange.

113 Grange, P. (2021). *Fear Less: How to win your way in work and life*. Vermilion, pp. 21–4.

114 Grange 2021, p. 29.

115 Pippa Grange in Brené Brown's *Dare to Lead* podcast interview 2021: Grange, P. (29 Mar. 2021). On fearing less. Retrieved from https://brenebrown.com/podcast/brene-with-dr-pippa-grange-on-fearing-less/.

116 Wilma Murto was interviewed by YLE, the Finnish Public Broadcasting, on 17 August 2023: https://yle.fi/a/74-2004 4060. Translation by the author.

117 Quote from the same article as above.

118 More about Appius Claudius Caecus can be found, for example, here: Britannica (n.d.). Appius Claudius Caecus. Retrieved from https://www.britannica.com/biography/Appius-Claudius-Caecus.

119 Peter D. (15 Oct. 2017). Social inequalities explained in a $100 race [video]. YouTube. Retrieved from https://www.youtube.com/watch?v=4K5fbQ1-zps&t=1s.

Chapter 7: The Centre of Indifference

120 E! Insider (10 Sep. 2017). Jim Carrey sounds off on icons and more at NYFW 2017 | E! red carpet & award shows [video]. YouTube. Retrieved from https://youtu.be/-JmNKGfFj7w?si=C4G3kTcECcky8fqG ; after the interview, Jim Carrey sent flowers, as reported by Catt Sadler in this interview: Virgin Radio Dubai (12 Oct. 2017). Jim Carey sent Catt Sadler something after the Bizarre Viral Interview [video]. YouTube. Retrieved from https://www.youtube.com/watch?v=jGgjiB-ZDlg.

121 Tolstoy, L. My confession (Wierner, L. trans.). In: Klemke, E. D. (ed.). *The Meaning of Life* (2nd edition). Oxford University Press, pp. 11–20 (p. 15).

122 Thoreau, H. (n.d.). I am a parcel of vain strivings tied.

Poetry Foundation. Retrieved from https://www.poetry foundation.org/poems/4627 1/i-am-a-parcel-of-vain-strivings -tied.

123 The famous line is found in Act 5, Scene 5 of *Macbeth*. Shakespeare, W. (1907). *The Tragedy of Macbeth*. Morang Educational Company, p. 99.

124 Carlyle, T. (1991). *Sartor Resartus*. Oxford University Press. I write about Carlyle's book and its influence in Martela (2023).

125 Gilmour, R. (1993). *The Victorian Period: The intellectual and cultural context of English literature 1830–1890*. Logman Group, p. 28.

126 Carlyle (1991), p. 127.

127 Epictetus. Discourses. In: Long, A. A. (ed.). *How to be Free: An ancient guide to the Stoic life*. Princeton University Press, pp. 100–51 (p. 147).

128 Peirce wrote this definition for *Century Dictionary* (1889–91). See Bergman, M. (2015). Minimal Meliorism: Finding a balance between conservative and progressive pragmatism. In: Zackariasson, U. (ed.). *Action, Belief and Inquiry—Pragmatist perspectives on science, society and religion* (Vol. 2). Nordic Pragmatism Network, pp. 2–28.

129 Greta Thunberg's story is told in many articles. My main sources were: BBC News (30 Dec. 2019). Greta Thunberg's father: 'She is happy, but I worry'. Retrieved from https://www.bbc.com/news/uk-50901789; BBC News (9 May 2024). Greta Thunberg: Who is the climate activist and what has she achieved? Retrieved from https://www.bbc.com/news/world-europe-49918719.

130 Quote from the same article as above.

131 Frankl (1985), p. 127.

132 The lines are from Eino Leino's poem 'Hymni Tulelle, Ode to the Fire'. A translation can be found here: Moreton, R. (14 Nov. 2015). Hymn to the Fire (Hymni tulelle), Eino Leino. Lingua Fennica. Retrieved from https://linguafennica.wordpress.com/2015/11/14/hymn-to-the-fire-hymni-tulelle-eino-leino.

Chapter 8: Start Caring About Yourself

133 Note that Sally Salminen wrote in Swedish, which was the native language of people of Åland, even though the island is part of Finland. The quotes in this and the next paragraph are from this article: Garrott, G. B. (16 Oct. 1936). Maid spent a year writing prize book. *New York Times*, pp. 1 and 12.

134 The following Finnish-language newspaper article has been used as one of the major sources

on Sally Salminen's life story: Pallaste, T. (6 Jul. 2019). Suuri tuntematon. *Helsingin Sanomat.*

135 Quote from the *New York Times* article referenced above.

136 The translations into English are my own. Salminen, S. (2023). *Katrina.* Hurme, J. (trans.). Teos.

137 Woolf, V. (20 Nov. 1919). George Eliot. *The Times Literary Supplement.*

138 David (2016), p. 143.

139 Pallaste (2019).

140 Sartre (2007), p. 29.

141 Stanovich, K. E. (2005). *The Robot's Rebellion: Finding meaning in the age of Darwin.* University of Chicago Press.

142 Chang, R. (May 2014). How to make hard choices [video]. TEDSalon. Retrieved from https://www.ted.com/talks/ ruth_chang_how_to_make_ hard_choices/.

143 See Neff, K. D. (2011). Self-compassion, self-esteem, and well-being. *Social and Personality Psychology Compass,* *5*(1), pp. 1–12; Neff, K. D. (2023). Self-compassion: Theory, method, research, and intervention. *Annual Review of Psychology, 74,* pp. 193–218.

144 Neff, K. D. (2003). Self-compassion: An alternative conceptualization of a healthy attitude toward oneself. *Self and Identity, 2*(2), pp. 85–101.

145 Neff (2023), p. 201.

146 The references for the studies mentioned in this paragraph can be found in Neff (2023); see, for example, these two meta-analyses: Zessin, U., Dickhäuser, O., and Garbade, S. (2015). The relationship between self-compassion and well-being: A meta-analysis. *Applied Psychology: Health and Well-Being, 7*(3), pp. 340–64; Luo, X., et al. (2021). Investigating the influence of self-compassion-focused interventions on post-traumatic stress: A systematic review and meta-analysis. *Mindfulness, 12*(12), pp. 2865–76.

147 Hiraoka, R., et al. (2015). Self-compassion as a prospective predictor of PTSD symptom severity among trauma-exposed U.S., Iraq and Afghanistan war veterans. *Journal of Traumatic Stress, 28*(2), pp. 127–33; Dahm, K. A., et al. (2015). Mindfulness, self-compassion, posttraumatic stress disorder symptoms, and functional disability in U.S., Iraq and Afghanistan war veterans. *Journal of Traumatic Stress, 28*(5), pp. 460–4.

148 Dundas, I., et al. (2017). Does a short self-compassion intervention for students increase healthy self-regulation? A randomized control trial.

Scandinavian Journal of Psychology, *58*(5), pp. 443–50; Zhang, J. W., and Chen, S. (2016). Self-compassion promotes personal improvement from regret experiences via acceptance. *Personality and Social Psychology Bulletin*, *42*(2), pp. 244–58.

149 Neff (2023), p. 202.

150 For example, Swee, M. B., et al. (2023). A brief self-compassionate letter-writing intervention for individuals with high shame. *Mindfulness*, *14*(4), pp. 854–67; Johnson, E. A., and O'Brien, K. A. (2013). Self-compassion soothes the savage EGO-threat system: Effects on negative affect, shame, rumination, and depressive symptoms. *Journal of Social and Clinical Psychology*, *32*(9), pp. 939–63. For a review, see Neff (2023).

151 See the vast amount of research about autonomy as a psychological need done within self-determination theory. Ryan, R. M., and Deci, E. L. (2000). Self-determination theory and the facilitation of intrinsic motivation, social development, and well-being. *American Psychologist*, *55*(1), pp. 68–78; Martela, F., and Ryan, R. M. (2023). Clarifying eudaimonia and psychological functioning to complement evaluative and experiential well-being – Why basic psychological needs should be measured in national accounts of well-being. *Perspectives on Psychological Science*, *18*(5), pp. 1121–35.

152 Järvilehto, L. (2014). *Learning As Fun*. Rovio Learning.

153 See Cohen, G. L., et al. (2006). Reducing the racial achievement gap: A social-psychological intervention. *Science*, *313*(5791), pp. 1307–131; Nelson, S. K., et al. (2014). Beyond self-protection: Self-affirmation benefits hedonic and eudaimonic well-being. *Personality and Social Psychology Bulletin*, *40*(8), pp. 998–1011.

154 Again, see self-determination theory for research on this need, for example Ryan and Deci (2000).

155 Quoted in Brim, G. (2016). *Ambition—How we manage success and failure throughout our lives*. iUniverse, p. 4.

156 International Olympic Committee (n.d.). What is the Olympic creed? Retrieved from https://olympics.com/ioc/faq/olympic-symbol-and-identity/what-is-the-olympic-creed.

157 Brim (2016), p. xiii.

158 In the first pages of his book: Brim (2016).

Chapter 9: Start Caring About Others

159 This research is reviewed in, for example, Baumeister, R. F.,

and Leary, M. R. (1995). The
need to belong: Desire for
interpersonal attachments
as a fundamental human
motivation. *Psychological
Bulletin, 117*(3), pp. 497–529.

160 I review these need theories in
Martela, F. (2024). Being as
having, loving, and doing: A
theory of human well-being.
*Personality and Social Psychology
Review*. Advance online
publication.

161 Baumeister, R. F., and
Tierney, J. (2011). *Willpower:
Rediscovering the greatest human
strength*. Penguin Press, p.6.

162 See Topping, A. (8 Aug. 2011).
Looting 'fuelled by social
exclusion'. *Guardian*. Retrieved
from https://www.theguardian.
com/uk/2011/aug/08/looting-
fuelled-by-social-exclusion.

163 Wuthnow, R. (1991). *Acts of
Compassion: Caring for others
and helping ourselves*. Princeton
University Press, p. 22.

**Chapter 10: Start Caring About
Building a Better World**

164 Coined by developmental
psychologist Jeffrey Arnett,
emerging adulthood has
generated much debate and
research in the last two decades:
Arnett, J. J. (2000). Emerging
adulthood: A theory of
development from the late teens
through the twenties. *American
Psychologist, 55*(5), pp. 469–80;

see also Henig, R. M.
(18 Aug. 2010). What is it
about 20-somethings? *New York
Times*. Retrieved from https://
www.nytimes.com/2010/08/22/
magazine/22Adulthood-t.html.

165 Demonstrating this would be a
long discussion touching upon
psychological research, primate
research and evolutionary
studies, so I just give a few
references here to start the
conversation: Warneken, F.,
and Tomasello, M. (2009).
The roots of human altruism.
*British Journal of Psychology,
100*(3), pp. 455–71; Fehr, E.,
and Fischbacher, U. (2003).
The nature of human altruism.
Nature, 425, pp. 785–91;
West, S. A., Griffin, A. S.,
and Gardner, A. (2007).
Evolutionary explanations
for cooperation. *Current
Biology, 17*(16), pp. R661–72;
Barclay, P., and van Vugt, M.
(2015). The evolutionary
psychology of human
prosociality: Adaptations,
byproducts, and mistakes. In:
Schroeder, D. A., and Graziano,
W. G. (eds.). *The Oxford
Handbook of Prosocial Behavior*.
Oxford University Press,
pp. 37–60.

166 See empirical research by me
and others: Martela, F., and
Ryan, R. M. (2016). Prosocial
behavior increases well-being
and vitality even without

contact with the beneficiary: Causal and behavioral evidence. *Motivation and Emotion*, *40*(3), pp. 351–7; Martela, F., et al. (2021). What makes work meaningful? Longitudinal evidence for the importance of autonomy and beneficence for meaningful work. *Journal of Vocational Behavior*, *131*(103631), pp. 1–15; Van Tongeren, D. R., et al. (2016). Prosociality enhances meaning in life. *The Journal of Positive Psychology*, *11*(3), pp. 225–36; Klein, N. (2017). Prosocial behavior increases perceptions of meaning in life. *The Journal of Positive Psychology*, *12*(4), pp. 354–61.

167 Crocker and Nuer (2003).

168 See, for example, Martela, F., and Ryan, R. M. (2021). If giving money to the Red Cross increases well-being, does taking money from the Red Cross increase ill-being? – Evidence from three experiments. *Journal of Research in Personality*, *93*(104114), pp. 1–10; Aknin, L. B., at al. (2013). Prosocial spending and well-being: Cross-cultural evidence for a psychological universal. *Journal of Personality and Social Psychology*, *104*(4), pp. 635–52; Hui, B. P. H., et al. (2020). Rewards of kindness? A meta-analysis of the link between prosociality and well-being. *Psychological Bulletin*, *146*(12), pp. 1084–116.

169 Carlyle (1991), p. 148. For the context and reception of the book, see my article on the topic: Martela (2023).

170 Carlyle (1991, p. 148.

171 Carlyle (1991), p. 93.

172 Moore, C. (1955). *Sartor Resartus* and the problem of Carlyle's conversion. *Publications of the Modern Language Association of America*, pp. 662–81 (p. 673).

173 Preface to the 1984 edition. In: Frankl (1985), pp. 16–17.

174 Most of the sources on Ryti's story are in Finnish. The few sources I used include the following: Henkilöhistoria (n.d.). Ryti, Risto (1889–1956). Retrieved from https://kansallisbiografia.fi/kansallisbiografia/henkilo/630.

175 Cited here (in Finnish, translation by the author): https://www.presidenttiristoryti.fi/elama-ja-ura/sotasyyllisyys-ja-vankila.

176 Belli, G. (2003). *The Country Under My Skin*. Anchor Books, p. 91.

177 Carlyle, T. (1872). *On Heroes, Hero-Worship and the Heroic in History*. Chapman and Hall, p. 149.

Conclusion: The Delicate Art of Not Caring, While Caring Deeply

178 The story is told, for example, in this newspaper article (in Finnish): https://www.is.fi/makihyppy/art-2000006016593.html.

179 Nagel, T. (1987). *What Does It All Mean? A Very Short Introduction to Philosophy.* Oxford University Press, p. 101.

180 Galbraith, E. D., et al. (2024). High life satisfaction reported among small-scale societies with low incomes. *Proceedings of the National Academy of Sciences, 121*(7), p. e2311703121.

181 Epicurus (1964). *Letters, Principal Doctrines, and Vatican Sayings.* Geer, R. (trans.). Merrill, p. 68.

182 Quoted in Pietikäinen, H.-P. (2019). *Työelämän taktiikkataulu – Huippu-urheiluvalmennuksen opit ja mahdollisuudet.* Fitra, p. 178.

183 Juurikkala (2024), p. 212.

184 The whole speech can be found here: Theodore Roosevelt Center (n.d.). The man in the arena. Retrieved from https://www.theodorerooseveltcenter.org/Learn-About-TR/TR-Encyclopedia/Culture-and-Society/Man-in-the-Arena.aspx.

185 Brady, T. (21 May 2020). X. Retrieved from https://x.com/TomBrady/status/1263513066907619335.

186 Tabermann, T. (2019). Eksymättä et löydä perille. Gummerus, p. 13. (Translation by the author.)

187 I recently heard that there is a word for this – *sonder*, defined by John Koenig in his *The Dictionary of Obscure Sorrows*, as 'the realization that each random passerby is living a life as vivid and complex as your own'.

188 Jasu was interviewed in this newspaper article: Kuokkanen, K. (26 Oct. 2008) Joku voisi sanoa pummi, mutta olen vielä hengissä. *Helsingin Sanomat.* Translation by the author.